SINGER

SEWING REFERENCE LIBRARY™

Sewing Specialty Fabrics

SINGER

SEWING REFERENCE LIBRARY™

Sewing Specialty Fabrics

Contents

How to Use This Book 7

Special Occasion Fabrics. 41

Lace & Embroidered 42	**Lustrous 53**
How Laces Are Sold 44	Techniques 54
Techniques for Sewing . . . 46	Hems 55
Seams 48	Closures 56
Hem & Edge Finishes . . . 50	Sequined & Metallic
Lace Appliqué 52	Fabrics 58

Classic Fabrics 61

Loose Weaves 64	Gabardine 74
Corduroy & Velveteen . . . 66	Large Prints 75
Velvet 68	Plaids & Stripes 76
Diagonal Designs 72	

Copyright © 1986
Cy DeCosse Incorporated
5900 Green Oak Drive
Minnetonka, Minnesota 55343
All rights reserved

Additional volumes in the Singer Sewing
Reference Library are available from the
publisher:
   Sewing Essentials
   Sewing for the Home
   Clothing Care & Repair
   Sewing for Style

Library of Congress Cataloging in
Publication Data

Sewing Specialty Fabrics

(Singer Sewing Reference Library)
Includes index.
1. Textile Fabrics. 2. Sewing. I. Series.
TT557.S49 1985 646.11 85-13050
ISBN 0-86573-209-4
ISBN 0-86573-210-8 (pbk.)

Distributed by: Random House, Inc.
ISBN 0-394-74416-0

CY DE COSSE INCORPORATED
Chairman: Cy DeCosse
President: James B. Maus
Executive Vice President: William B. Jones

SEWING SPECIALTY FABRICS
Created by: The Editors of Cy DeCosse
  Incorporated, in cooperation with the
  Singer Education Department. Singer is a
  trademark of The Singer Company and is
  used under license.

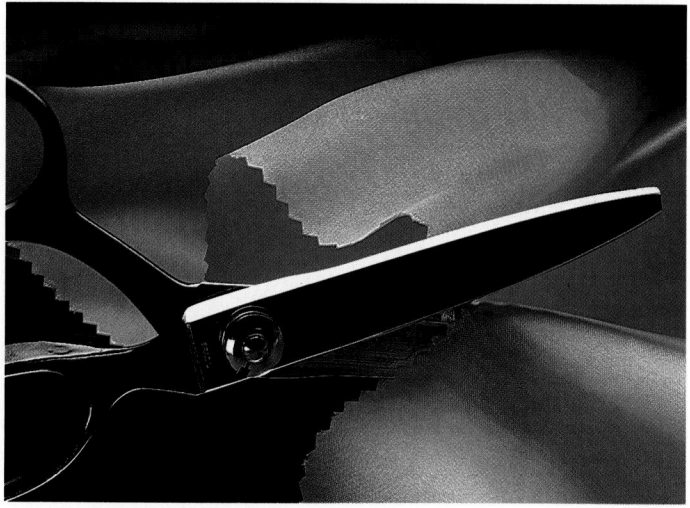

Getting Started 9
Sewing Equipment 12
Layout & Cutting Equipment 14
Pressing Equipment 16
Marking Tools 17

Sheer & Silky Fabrics 19
Techniques . . . . 22 Bindings & Underlinings 29
Interfacings . . . . 24 Set-in Sleeves 33
Marking & Stitching . . . . . 25 Hidden Plackets 34
Seams . . . . 26 Narrow Hems 36

Fabulous Fakes 83
Synthetic Fur . . . . 86 Synthetic Suede 90
Hems . . . . 88 Conventional Techniques 92
Closures . . . . 89 Flat Techniques 93
                                     Closures 98
                                Vinyl 102

Knits 105
Techniques . . . . 108 Edge Finishes 114
Selecting Needle, Stitch   Elasticized Waistbands &
Length & Thread . . . . . . 110 Cuffs 118
Stabilizing Seams . . . . . . 112 Plackets 120
Hems . . . . 113 Two-way Stretch Knits . . 123

Managing Editor: Reneé Dignan
Project Director: Gail Devens
Senior Art Director: Susan Schultz
Art Director: James Olson
Editors: Susan Meyers, Bernice Maehren
Writer: Peggy Bendel
Sample Supervisor: Carol Neumann
Fabric Editor: Rita Opseth
Sewing Staff: Phyllis Galbraith, Bridget
  Haugh, Sheila Duffy, Kathleen Davis
  Ellingson, Wendy Fedie, Rebecca Hanson,
  Jeanine Theroux

Photographers: Kris Boom, Jerry Krause,
  Tony Kubat, Jerry Robb
Production Consultant: Christine Watkins
Production Manager: Jim Bindas
Assistant Production Manager: Julie Churchill
Production Staff: Michelle Alexander, Yelena
  Konrardy, Nancy Nardone, Jennie Smith,
  Bryan Trandem, Nik Wogstad
Consultants: Kathleen Alme, LaVern Bell,
  Karole Farley, Wendy Fedie, Joy Gerard,
  JoAnn Krause, Marilyn Miller, Rita
  Opseth, Ruth Reetz; Zoe Graul, The
  Singer Company

Contributing Manufacturers: B. Blumenthal &
  Co., Inc.; Borg Textile Corp.; Crown
  Textile Co.; Dan River, Inc.; Everitt
  Knitting Mills; Fine Velvet by J. B. Martin
  Company; House of Laird; Lamaire® by
  Uniroyal; Minnesota Fabrics, Inc.;
  Minnetonka Mills, Inc.; North America
  Taxidermy; Seams Great Products, Inc.;
  The Singer Company; South Sea
  Imports; Yarnell Fabrics Corp.
Color Separations: La Cromolito
Printing: R. R. Donnelley & Sons Co.

How to Use This Book

Choosing a fabric that is new or different makes sewing exciting. Yet, even experienced sewers may hesitate to work with a fabric that is unfamiliar, no matter how attractive it is. *Sewing Specialty Fabrics* is dedicated to removing that unsure feeling. This book contains up-to-date sewing methods, giving you confidence to create fashions from fabrics that you may never have used before.

Specialty Fabrics Defined

A specialty fabric may be distinctive because of its weight, texture, decorative design, or other special qualities. Many specialty fabrics are selected for a specific purpose such as bridal and evening wear, swimwear, active wear, or rainwear. Others are classics that people of all ages wear season after season.

A specialty fabric may require handling that differs from traditional sewing practices. The special handling may involve extra steps, such as making French seams or planning a unique pattern layout. Or it may mean taking shortcuts, such as omitting interfacings or topstitching hems.

Organized for Easy Reference

This book is organized to help you quickly find the information you need. First is an overview to help you in the early steps of sewing specialty fabrics. Use it as a guide for selecting patterns and equipment suited to specialty fabrics. Following this overview, the fabrics are conveniently grouped according to similar sewing techniques. The five sections include sheer and silky fabrics, special occasion fabrics, classic fabrics, synthetic furs and leathers, and knits.

Each of the five sections on specialty fabrics is independent of the others, so you will find in one place all the key facts about handling a fabric. At the beginning of each section is a swatch guide to help you identify the fabrics discussed in the section.

Anyone who has wondered what charmeuse, tissue faille, or galloon lace looks like will find this helpful.

Also at the start of each section, wherever appropriate, is a chart with basic needle, thread, stitch length, seam, and hem recommendations in capsule form. Use the chart as an introduction to the sewing methods for a specialty fabric. Then use it as a summary after you have studied the step-by-step directions on the pages that follow.

Expert Guidance

Within each section you will find information on pattern selection, fabric preparation, pattern layout, cutting, marking, and pressing techniques. Helpful sewing aids, tools, and supplies are highlighted; these extras help simplify the work. Sewing methods for seams, hems, edges, and details are presented in a step-by-step format in color photographs whenever they are different from traditional sewing. When necessary, contrasting thread is used to make the stitches more visible in the photos. This is an illustrative technique, you will want to use matching thread in your own sewing.

Wherever possible, we have given you the choice of handling a special fabric with straight stitching only, with zigzag or special purpose stitches, or with an overlock (serger) technique. Select the method that suits your sewing equipment.

A Creative Adventure

While researching this book, we found many unusual fabrics available for sewing, and new ones continue to appear. We have included the most traditional and readily available fabrics, but you will surely discover others; we encourage you to try them. Put your creativity to work, testing sewing and pressing methods until you have found the best way to handle *your* special fabric.

Getting Started

Getting Started

A little planning in the early stages of sewing a specialty fabric can simplify your project and get it off to a smooth start. When you use a fabric that is distinctive, you want to highlight its special quality by choosing the right pattern, fitting it precisely, laying it out and cutting it accurately, and sewing the garment expertly. Work out the details for these four steps, and you will be happy with the results. With careful planning, you will continue to sew specialty fabrics with satisfaction and success.

Select a Pattern

Pairing suitable patterns and fabrics is always an important sewing decision. A rule of thumb fashion professionals use is the more distinctive the fabric, the simpler the pattern style. When a pattern has few seams and minimal detailing, the fabric becomes the focal point and carries the fashion style. If you have found an elaborate or highly decorative fabric to sew, such as re-embroidered lace, sequined chiffon, or a large print, look in the section of the pattern catalogs where easy-to-sew patterns are grouped. One of these patterns will probably suit your unusual fabric.

Throughout the pattern catalogs there are also patterns meant for use with specific fabrics. Some patterns are designed for sewing with two-way stretch knits only, for example. There are also patterns that can be used with a variety of fabrics, but are especially suitable for synthetic suede, synthetic fur, vinyl, galloon lace, plaids, stripes, or silkies. Check the suggested fabrics on the pattern envelope back to see if the fabric you wish to sew is mentioned.

Another good source of pattern ideas is ready-to-wear clothing. Designers frequently use specialty fabrics, so you will find examples in designer departments or specialty stores. Study these garments, and then look for similar patterns to sew. While you are window shopping for ideas, be sure to look inside the garments, too. You may discover a new sewing technique or a creative way to solve a construction problem.

Preview the Pattern

You may wish to preview the pattern you have selected by sewing it first in muslin, pattern tracing fabric, or an inexpensive fabric of similar weight. If working with a special fabric design, such as a large print, diagonal motif, or border, trace the outline of

Select an appropriate pattern. The more distinctive the fabric, the simpler the pattern should be.

Preview the pattern fit and appropriateness by sewing a fitting shell in an inexpensive fabric.

the fabric design or major motifs on the test fabric. If working with stripes or plaids, use large gingham checks for the pattern preview. The checks are similar to the crosswise and lengthwise bars of a plaid, or the bars of a stripe, so you can judge the overall effect.

Use a test garment to adjust the fit and to establish hemlines. Many specialty fabrics cannot be altered midway through construction without damage, either because pressing makes permanent creases or because ripped-out stitches weaken the fibers. A trial garment helps prevent mistakes and gives you confidence to work on expensive fashion fabrics.

Study the test garment and the pattern pieces to determine which garment areas require adapting. For example, when working with a bulky fabric such as synthetic fur or wide wale corduroy, cut hidden pattern sections such as facings or undercollars from lining fabric to eliminate bulk. Some pattern pieces, such as a front facing, can be lapped on the seam-line to omit the seam and simplify the sewing. Pockets and other details may be eliminated.

Lay Out the Pattern

After testing the pattern and making adjustments to the pattern pieces, you may need to make your own pattern layout before buying the fabric. Your layout may require less fabric than indicated on the back of the pattern envelope. If the fabric is costly, even ⅛ yard (.15 m) less can represent a significant savings. Some fabrics, such as velvet, come in unusual widths not commonly listed on patterns. Your own layout plan can give you an accurate estimate for fabric needs.

Use a folding cardboard cutting surface, or mark off the fabric width on paper or gingham as a substitute for the fabric. Position the pattern pieces for the most economical use of the fabric, arranging the printed grainline arrows carefully.

Practice Special Techniques

The final consideration before you are ready to start your special garment is to adjust the sewing machine for the fabric. Test stitch quality with fabric scraps left over from cutting out the pattern. Adjust stitch length, stitch width, tension, and pressure. If you encounter stitching problems, try a different needle type or size. Changing to a different thread, presser foot, or throat plate may be necessary for a satisfactory, balanced stitch. Consult the sewing machine manual if setting up the machine for special stitches or functions.

When sewing a specialty fabric for the first time, try special seams and hems on fabric scraps. Even experienced dressmakers test techniques for seams, hems, and buttonholes before deciding which method to use on a garment. Investing this time beforehand can save time and frustration later. When there are several methods recommended, try more than one to see which one you prefer. Experiment on your own to find a better or faster way to sew the fabric you have chosen.

Practice pressing techniques on scraps, too. See if the fabric spots from water; if so, do not use steam to press. Determine the best temperature setting on the iron, beginning at the low end of the dial and advancing to a higher level as needed. Check results on the right and wrong side of the fabric.

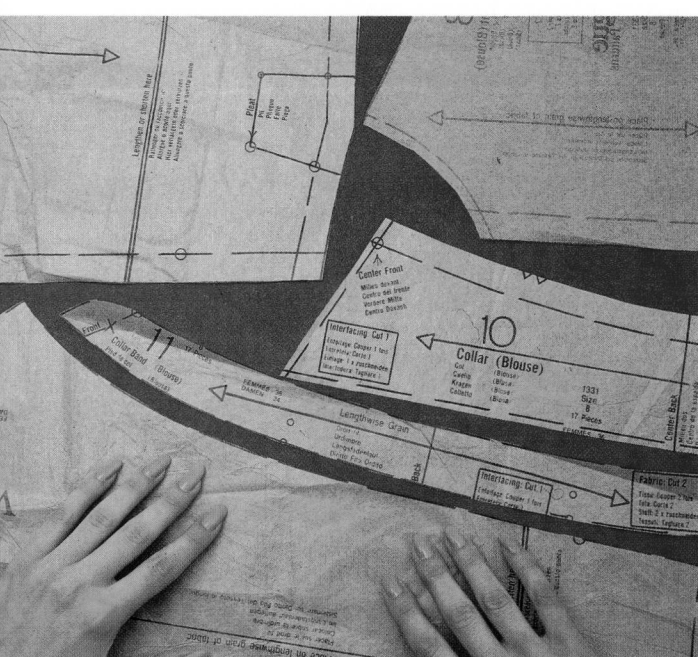

Try the layout. Position the pattern pieces for the most economical use of the fabric.

Adjust the sewing machine. Test stitch quality and seam and buttonhole techniques. Insert new needle.

Sewing Equipment

You can handle specialty fabrics without investing in an elaborate sewing machine. Wherever appropriate throughout this book, instructions include three ways to accomplish a special sewing method: straight stitching alone, zigzag or special-purpose stitching, or overlock stitching on a three or four-thread overlock machine (serger). An overlock machine feeds thin, sheer, slippery, bulky, and loosely woven or knit fabrics evenly and naturally without any special attachments. Overlock techniques give you professional-looking results and save time by eliminating the need to trim seam allowances or sew additional edge finishes.

Whether your sewing machine is new or old, top of the line or basic, and whether or not you are using an overlock machine, you will find a suitable technique given. Helpful accessories such as special feet for the sewing machine are used whenever appropriate; these are available for most machines.

Whatever sewing equipment you have, prepare for stitching on special fabrics by cleaning and oiling the machine and making sure you have a supply of new needles on hand. Working on a machine that is in good condition prevents many stitching problems. Consult your machine manual for the location of lubrication points. Newer machines require oil on the bobbin hook only; older machines require oil at several key points. Most overlocks have a self-lubricating wick system where oil is applied to the wick and the metal-to-metal parts under the bed of the machine.

Machine Thread & Needles

Purchase fine sewing thread in economy sizes for overlock machines, which use three or four spools of thread at a time. Large cones (1) hold up to 6,000 yards (5,485 m). Smaller cones (2) hold up to 1,000 yards (914 m). Tubes (3) hold up to 1,700 yards (1,554 m). These threads can be used on conventional machines by using plastic or metal adapters (4) as thread holders. Other types of threads are also available for overlock machines.

Choose conventional machine thread according to needle size and fabric weight. All-purpose thread (5) fits needle sizes 11 (75) and above. Topstitching and buttonhole twist (6) fits size 16 (100) needle for decorative accent stitching. Extra-fine thread (7) fits size 9 (65) needle and is used on thin, delicate fabrics as well as for machine embroidery and satin stitching.

Select needle size and type according to fabric type and weight. Sharp points (8) are used for woven and nonwoven fabrics. Ballpoints (9) are used for knits. Universal points (10) can be used for many fabric types, knitted and woven. Twin needle (11) is used for stitching two closely spaced parallel rows at a time. It can be used only on zigzag machines.

Even Feed™ **foot** attachment draws upper layer of fabric under needle at same rate as lower layer. Use it for fabrics such as vinyl, synthetic suede, sheers, slippery fabrics, and bulky knits, which tend to stick, slide, or stretch.

Roller foot has metal rollers that ride over textured fabrics to help them feed evenly without leaving an imprint. Use on napped or slippery fabrics, such as velveteen, corduroy, and synthetic suede.

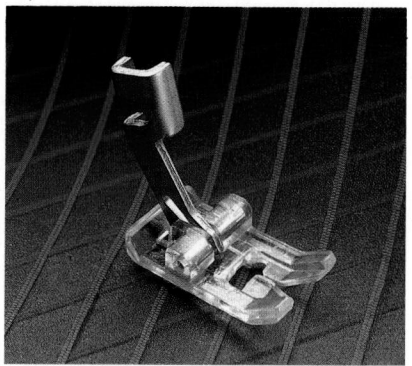

Special-purpose foot is clear plastic for better visibility with stretch and embroidery stitches. Groove underneath foot allows for thread buildup for raised stitches, such as satin stitching and hairline seams on sheer fabrics.

Zipper foot allows you to sew next to raised edge, such as zipper coil. This foot adjusts to either side of needle. Position zipper foot so stitches are next to coil but do not interfere with zipper slide.

Overedge foot has hook on inside edge. Stitches form over hook, so fabric edges do not curl and stitches are full width without puckers. Use for zigzag overcasting and for special overedge stitch patterns.

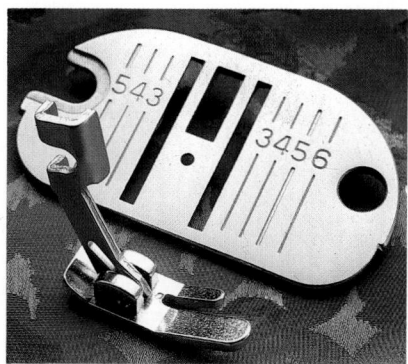

Straight-stitch throat plate and straight-stitch foot prevent stitches and fabric from being drawn down into the opening.

Narrow hemmer scrolls fabric automatically. This eliminates time-consuming pressing and pinning of narrow hems on sheers and silkies. Foot folds fabric twice so stitches form ⅛" (3 mm) from finished hem edge.

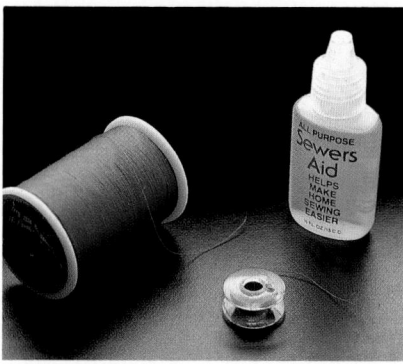

Silicone lubricant is used on spool and bobbin threads to aid smooth stitching and prevent skipped stitches. One drop treats entire spool of thread. Also use on presser foot and throat plate for stitching fabrics that resist even feeding.

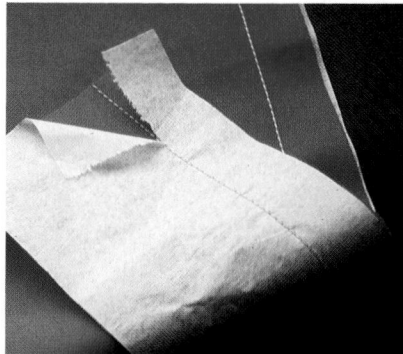

Tissue paper or tear-away paper stabilizes sheers, slippery satins, and silkies. Place strip of tissue over or under the fabric on the seamline. Tissue paper is appropriate weight for easy needle penetration and tears off easily.

Layout & Cutting Equipment

A number of items are helpful for laying out and cutting a pattern on specialty fabrics. Some of the supplies and equipment are major purchases and may already be part of your collection. Others are minor purchases and worth the small expense, especially when you are working on luxury-priced specialty fabrics.

1) Pattern tracing fabric serves a dual purpose. Because many specialty fabrics are easier to handle in a single layer for pattern layout, use tracing fabric to make a complete or duplicate pattern piece. Trace pattern pieces on tracing fabric, duplicating pieces that are cut twice. This saves time in the long run whenever you cut a single layer of fabric. Pattern tracing fabric can also be used to test-fit a garment. Machine-baste the tracing fabric pattern together to test the fit; mark any changes before cutting into the fashion fabric. This can prevent damage from ripped-out stitches.

2) Superfine pins (.5 mm) are less likely than dressmaker pins to damage finely woven silky fabric. To prevent tiny black pin spots, wipe the oil coating off before using the pins for the first time.

3) Silk pins with glass or plastic heads are easy to grasp and see. Use on light to mediumweight fabrics.

4) Long pins (4a) and quilting pins (4b) are useful for loose weaves, thick or bulky fabrics, and synthetic furs. Shorter pins can get lost in these fabrics.

5) Weights are a useful sewing aid and save time during pattern layout and cutting. Use them for fabrics such as vinyl, which can be damaged by pins.

6) Masking tape is an aid for laying out patterns on sequined fabrics. To prevent loss of sequins on cut edges, leave the tape in place after cutting.

7) Bent-handled shears help you cut accurately, especially if the fabric is slippery, sheer, or tightly woven. The lower blade rests on the work surface as you cut, so the fabric does not have to be lifted off the table and it will be less likely to shift or slide.

8) Serrated-edge shears give maximum control on slippery fabrics. The serrated blade grips the fabric and helps prevent jagged cut edges.

9) Rotary cutter, always used with a protective cutting mat under the fabric, cuts sharp, clean edges. This is especially beneficial for slippery fabrics, fine sheers, and synthetic suedes.

10) Single-edged razor blade (10a) or knife blade cutting tool (10b) is used to cut bulky synthetic fur. The blade slices through the backing without damaging the pile on the right side of the fur.

11) Buttonhole cutter and block is a chisel tool that aids in cutting open machine-made buttonholes with a single sharp slice between the stitching rows.

Pressing Equipment

Pressing as you sew is important for specialty fabrics, but an equally important principle is to *avoid too much pressing*. Many of these fabrics are easily damaged by heat and steam. Fine fabrics such as silks and silky synthetics are quickly penetrated by heat and require only a light touch during construction pressing. Without this light touch, seams leave imprints on the right side of the garment or the fabric scorches and draws up into permanent wrinkles.

Vinyl, synthetic furs, and sequined and metallic fabrics should not be steam pressed. Heat melts the fibers, and steam removes the surface luster. Simple finger pressing with a thimble or the blunt end of a point turner is often the best approach.

For textured pile fabrics, such as velvet, velveteen, and corduroy, press lightly so the plush surface is preserved. Do not press down on the iron.

1) Steam/spray iron is essential sewing equipment. When pressing specialty fabrics, begin with a low temperature setting, and raise the temperature as needed for desired results. Keep the iron clean and in good condition. If the soleplate has nicks or scratches, delicate fabrics may be snagged.

2) Hand steamer provides a cloud of steam at a low temperature setting. Although a steamer will not produce enough heat for permanent fusing, it holds fusible web in place temporarily for the special construction methods used on synthetic suede. A steamer can also be used on the right side of velvet and other pile or heat-sensitive fabrics.

3) Press cloth protects fabrics from too much heat and steam. In general, use a press cloth whenever pressing on the right side of a fabric. Also use a press cloth when pressing on the wrong side of lace or other fragile fabrics.

4) Iron soleplate cover attaches to the bottom of any iron to prevent scorching and shine on fabrics. It may be used in place of a press cloth for safe pressing on delicate and napped fabrics.

5) Needle board has flexible bed of steel needles, which are angled so the pile of a fabric falls between needles for pressing. Use a needle board to prevent crushing or matting velvets and plush fabric textures.

6) Seam roll is a firm cushion used to press seams open without leaving imprints. The seam allowances and bulk of the garment section fall to the sides of the seam roll, and the iron touches only the seam itself during pressing.

7) Point presser/clapper does dual duty. As a hardwood pressing surface, it enables you to press open enclosed seams, even at tight corners and points. As a clapper, it forces steam into hard-surfaced fabrics to flatten seams and edges.

Marking Tools

Transferring pattern markings to cutout fabric sections requires out-of-the-ordinary marking methods on many specialty fabrics. As a general guideline, mark as little as possible. Transfer the essential dots and notches as you cut. Leave the rest unmarked. Use the tissue pattern to help position details such as patch pockets, hemlines, and buttonholes, placing the pattern tissue on the garment section as needed to mark the details.

If marking with water-soluble marking pen or pins and chalk, test the method on a fabric scrap first to check for stains or damage to the fabric. The shortcut marking method of cutting snips in the seam allowances is rarely appropriate for specialty fabrics; snips may weaken the fabric and interfere with special seam techniques.

1) Smooth-edged tracing wheel makes impressions on smooth-surfaced sheer or silky fabrics. These creases are sufficient to provide a temporary sewing guideline without the use of dressmaker's carbon paper. Avoid using a serrated tracing wheel on fine or delicate fabrics. Sharp points may pierce and weaken fibers.

2) Marking pen with disappearing ink works well on many specialty fabrics. This pen may be preferable to water-soluble marking pen because many specialty fabrics are not washable or are prone to water-spotting. Do not use marking pens on fabrics where the ink bleeds into the fabric texture instead of leaving a clear mark.

3) Tailor's chalk (3a) and chalk marking pencil (3b) make easy-to-remove marks on most fabrics. Some types of chalk leave permanent marks on silky fabric if pressed over; test on a fabric scrap before marking. Chalk also rubs off, or dissolves when steamed, so be careful not to erase chalk markings unless you no longer need them.

4) Thread is useful for tracing pattern markings onto delicate, open-textured fabrics such as lace. Use all-purpose thread or fine silk thread for this marking method; silk thread can be pressed over without leaving an imprint.

5) Transparent tape makes an excellent marking aid for lace, knits, and synthetic suede. When marking on the right side of the fabric, draw the stitching guidelines directly onto the tape with a pencil; after stitching, tear the tape away.

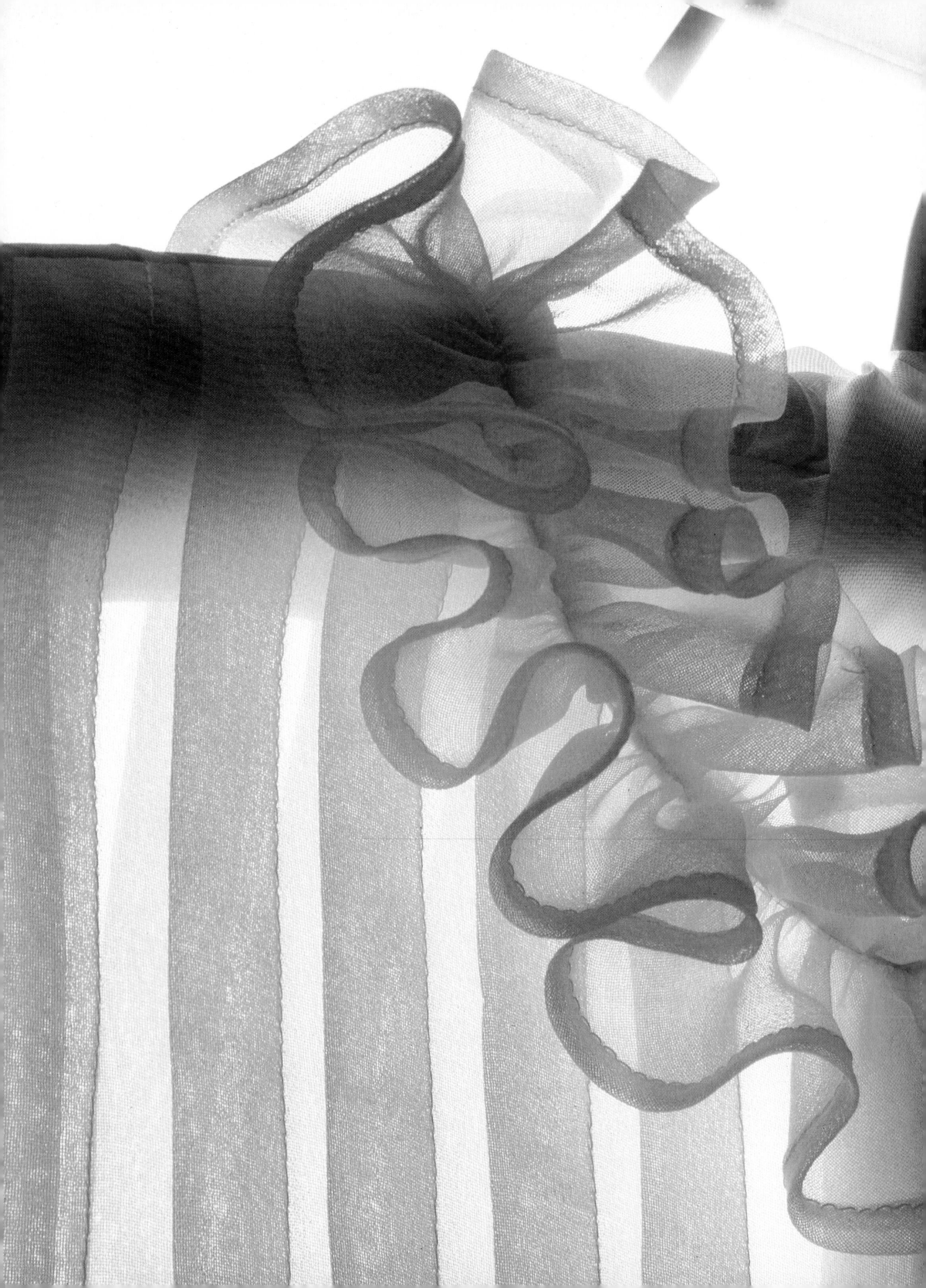

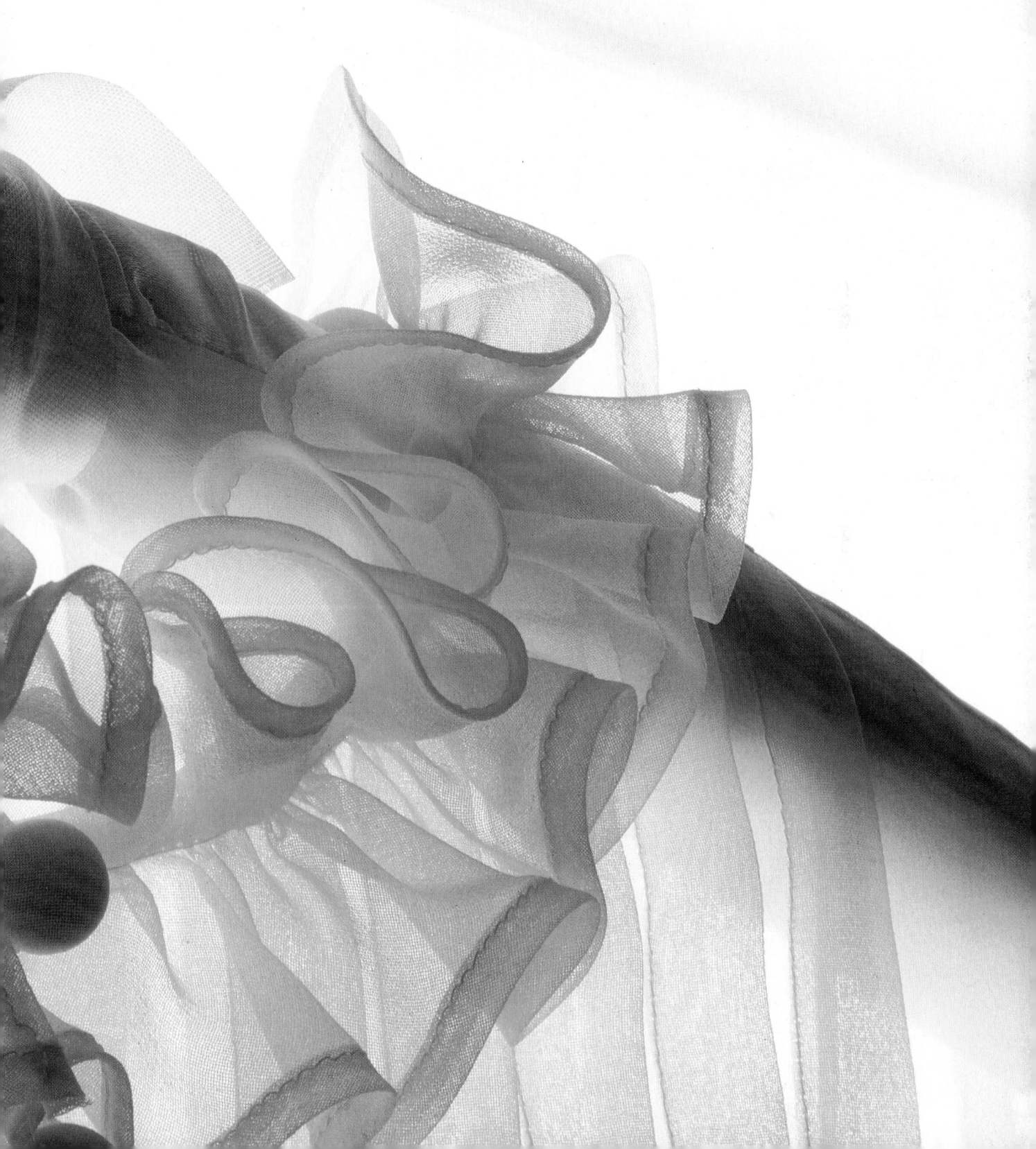

Sheer & Silky Fabrics

Sheer & Silky Fabrics

Sheer fabrics can have a soft or crisp hand; crisp sheers are easier to cut and sew. Soft sheers are batiste (1), chiffon (2), China silk (3), and georgette (4). Crisp sheers include fabrics such as organza (5), voile (6), and organdy (7).

The major consideration with sheer fabrics is their transparent quality. The stitches on the inside of a sheer garment show from the outside. Whether revealed clearly or as mere shadows, details such as seams, facings, and hems must be neat and narrow to look well made.

Silky fabrics are made from natural silk fibers or synthetic fibers that look like silk, such as polyester, nylon, rayon, and acetate. The polyester types are popular because they are less costly than silk fabrics. Most synthetic silk-like fabrics do not shrink or fade,

and can be washed and dried by machine. This group of fabrics includes charmeuse (8), crepe de chine (9), lightweight jacquard weaves (10), lightweight satin-backed crepe (11), and tissue faille (12).

Even when silk and synthetic silk-like fabrics do not have the see-through character of sheers, they do have similar fine weaves and light weights. Inner construction can show as ridges on the outside of silky garments. That is why many of the same sewing supplies and techniques are suggested for both kinds of fabrics. An additional consideration with silk-like fabrics is their smooth, slick texture, which makes them slippery to handle. You will need to take special steps when laying out and cutting the pattern pieces to control these fabrics.

Guide to Sewing Sheer and Silky Fabrics

Equipment & Techniques	Soft Sheers Batiste, chiffon, China silk, georgette **Crisp Sheers** Organdy, organza, voile	Lightweight Silkies Charmeuse, crepe de chine, jacquard weaves, satin-backed crepe, tissue faille
Machine Needles	Size 8 (60), 9 (65), or 11 (75)	Size 8 (60), 9 (65), or 11 (75)
Stitch Length	12 to 16 per inch (2.5 cm)	12 to 16 per inch (2.5 cm)
Millimeter Stitch Setting	2.5 to 2	2.5 to 2
Thread	Extra-fine long staple polyester; silk or mercerized cotton. These threads are often sold as notions for lingerie, machine embroidery, or quilting. Use finest thread possible.	
Hand Needles	Betweens, sizes 8 to 12	Betweens, sizes 8 to 12
Interfacings	Sheer nonwoven fusible or sew-in, self-fabric, organza	Fusible tricot, sheer nonwoven fusible or sew-in, batiste, self-fabric, lining fabric, organza, organdy
Special Seams	French, hairline, overlocked, double-stitched	French, overlocked, double-stitched
Special Hems	Overlocked, rolled overlocked, hand-rolled, tricot-bound, hairline, narrow topstitched	

Techniques for Sheer & Silky Fabrics

Keep in mind the delicate nature of sheer and silky fabrics when choosing patterns. The most suitable pattern designs are those that fit loosely and have graceful, flowing lines. Look for soft details such as gathers, ruffles, shirring, or draping. Crisp sheers, however, can be sewn from patterns with tailored, shirt-style details. Bias-cut pattern sections can be difficult to handle on silk and synthetic silk fabrics, which stretch a great deal as well as slip and slide.

For sheers, the fewer seams, darts, facings, and other details to sew, the less inside construction will show through to the right side. Also, the less time you will spend with special finishing techniques. Avoid patterns that require zippers, and omit in-seam pockets because zippers and pockets are bulky and can create an unattractive show-through on the outside of the garment.

Fabric Preparation

For best results, wash and dry sheer and silky fabrics before you begin working with them if they will be washed as part of their routine care. This preshrinks the fabric and removes resins, which can cause skipped stitches and make stitching difficult on synthetic fabrics. Follow the care instructions provided by the fabric manufacturer. Typical care instructions are to machine wash in a gentle cycle and tumble dry at a low temperature setting. Before washing, stitch along cut edges of the fabric to prevent excessive fraying.

Pure silk and silk/synthetic blend fabrics require special consideration. Silk fabrics can be drycleaned, but hand washing may be preferred. Warm water releases a natural substance from within the silk fibers, which renews the fabric and gives it a refreshed look. Prewashing also frees you from worry about water spotting. However, silk fabrics cannot be made colorfast, and dyes will run. Hand washing is not recommended for strong colors, prints, and iridescents but can be used for light solid colors. Use a sample of your fabric as a test to see how it reacts to hand washing; then prepare the entire length of fabric accordingly.

Also preshrink other fabrics, such as interfacings and linings. Even a tiny amount of shrinkage on these inner fabrics will show up as puckers or bubbles on thin, lightweight outer fabrics.

If you decide to dryclean your silk garment, prepare the fabric for sewing by steam pressing on the wrong side. Use a press cloth to protect the fabric. Set the iron at the lowest end of the steam setting.

Pressing

The best approach to pressing sheer and silky fabrics is to work with fabric scraps first. Determine

How to Hand Wash Silks

1) **Swish** fabric gently in lukewarm water. Use mild detergent, mild soap, or natural shampoo such as castile. Rinse in cool water.

2) **Roll** fabric in towel to remove excess moisture. Do not wring or twist; this causes wrinkles, which are difficult to remove.

3) **Press** on wrong side of fabric while it is wet. Use dry iron at cool temperature, such as synthetic setting, keeping grainlines true.

the optimum temperature setting on your iron, beginning with a low setting and raising it as needed. Fabrics made from rayon or polyester fibers scorch easily and require a cool iron temperature. Use a press cloth to protect fragile fabrics and fibers, or use a soleplate cover on your iron. Avoid a metal-coated ironing board cover because it reflects too much heat into the fabric.

Most pure silk fabrics can be pressed at a low steam setting, but test to see if steaming leaves spots. This is a hazard especially on pure silk fabrics that have not been prewashed before pattern layout and on lustrous fabrics such as charmeuse.

Avoid overpressing. Thin, lightweight fabrics are quickly penetrated by heat and need less pressing effort than heavier fabrics. A light touch is all that is necessary. Use a hand steamer on finished garments.

Layout & Cutting

In general, fine, lightweight fabrics are easier to handle during pattern layout if you cover the cutting surface with a sheet, other matte-surfaced fabric, or flannel-backed vinyl tablecloth with the flannel side up. Cardboard cutting boards and cork-covered or padded work surfaces also help to make slippery fabrics more controllable.

To pin patterns in position, use superfine pins (.5 mm diameter). They penetrate the fabric weave without marring it. Prepare new pins by wiping off the manufacturer's oil coating to prevent leaving spots, or use the pins first on dark fabric. In spite of their name, silk pins are too coarse for these fabrics and should be reserved for use with heavier fabrics such as raw silk.

The fastest way to cut out fine fabrics is with a rotary cutter. The blade cuts fabric edges neatly and does not shift the fabric as you work. Another good cutting tool is a bent-handled dressmaker's shears. The shape of the handle allows you to rest one cutting blade on the work surface for accurate strokes that barely disturb the fabric layers. Serrated-edge shears can also be helpful. The special blades firmly grip thin and slippery fabrics, a benefit not only for initial cutting but also for trimming raw edges. Whichever tool you use, be sure it is sharp; blades of shears should be in good alignment. Also, synthetic fabrics cause a fuzz buildup, which dulls the cutting blades; wipe this off with a soft cloth.

Use a "with nap" layout for all fabrics that have luster or shine. This one-way pattern layout guarantees uniform color shading in the finished garment. Some fabrics look lighter or brighter in one direction than the other; study the fabric before pattern layout and decide which shading you prefer.

Layout Techniques for Slippery Fabrics

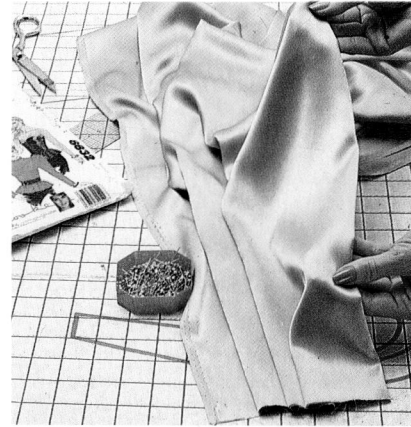

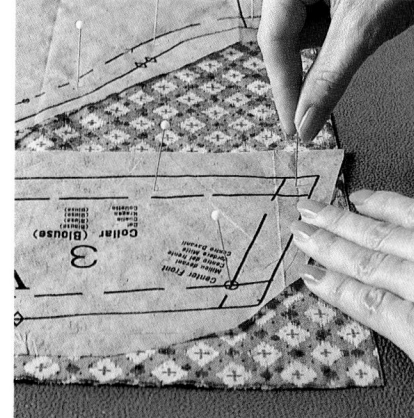

Fold fabric right side out, so less-slick wrong sides face each other. Pick up fabric along folded edge, and let fabric fall naturally to ensure accuracy of crosswise grain.

Push pins straight down through pattern seam allowance, fabric, and padded or cork-covered work surface to secure slippery layers. If using cardboard cutting board, avoid using superfine pins because cardboard dulls them quickly.

Sandwich extremely slippery or thin fabrics between two layers of tissue paper for better control. Place tissue paper on cutting board; place fabric and pattern on tissue; pin through all layers. Pin only in seam allowances.

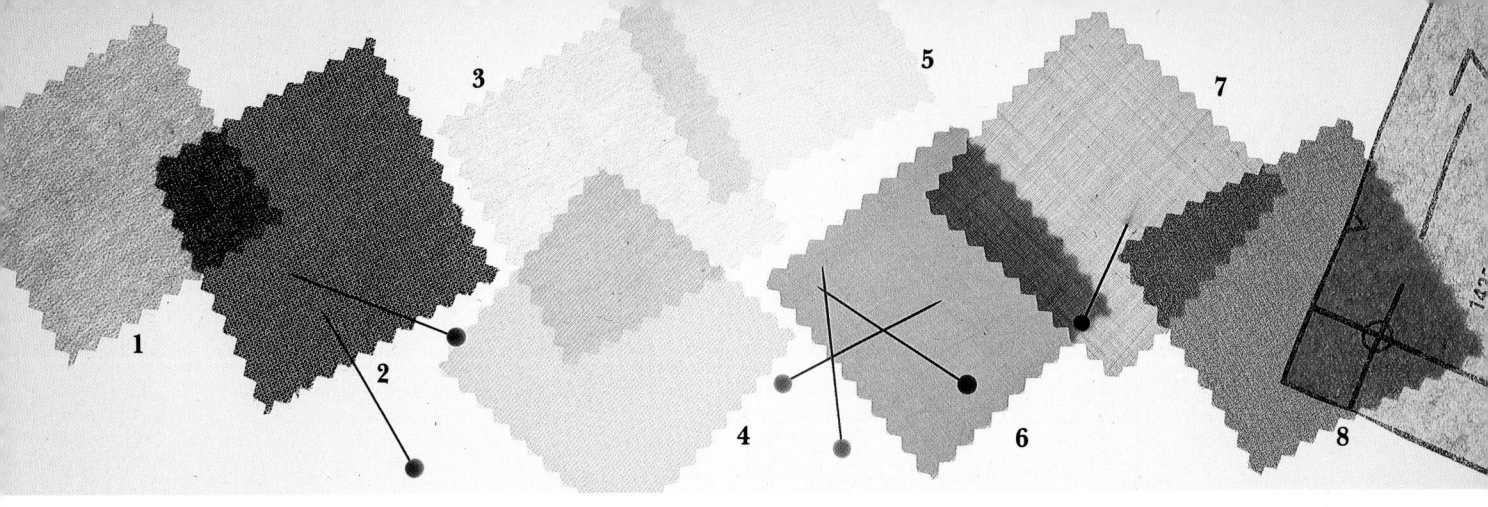

Interfacings

On sheer fabrics, interfacings must be equally sheer or they spoil the appearance of the garment by showing through to the outside. On silky fabrics, interfacings must blend with the soft fabric texture, adding body and support without adding stiffness. Similar interfacings work well for both types of fabrics. Interface collars and cuffs to hide enclosed seam allowances and to cushion the outer fabric, preventing ridges. Also interface buttoned closings to keep buttonholes from stretching and to provide a strong foundation for the buttons.

Choose interfacing that blends with the color and texture of the fabric without showing through to the right side. Suggested interfacings for delicate fabrics include sheer nonwoven fusible (1), fusible tricot (2), sheer nonwoven sew-in (3), polyester (4) or silk (5) organza, China silk (6) or other lining fabric, fine batiste or voile (7), and self-fabric (8).

Preshrink interfacings and linings. If you are using self-fabric or lining fabric as interfacing, your interfacing will have been preshrunk. If you are using another type of interfacing, prepare it with special handling as follows:

Woven or knit fusible. Soak in hot water for 10 minutes. Roll in a towel to remove excess moisture. Hang or lay flat to air dry.

Nonwoven fusible. Place interfacing, adhesive side down, on sheet or scrap fabric. Hold steam iron or hand steamer 1" to 2" (2.5 to 5 cm) above to shrink interfacing with moist heat. Let interfacing cool and dry before handling.

Silk organza. Hand wash and iron dry, following method for other silk fabrics.

Woven or nonwoven sew-in. Wash by machine and tumble dry.

Several sheer, nonwoven fusible interfacings have been developed especially for delicate fabrics. Some brands come in a selection of colors to blend with fabric colors and prints for minimal show-through on fashion sheers. Fusible tricot interfacing often adds just enough body to silky fabrics, although it is too opaque to use on sheers. Test all fusible interfacings on a fabric scrap before sewing. If the adhesive comes through to the right side of the fabric, use a sew-in interfacing.

Tips for Interfacing Delicate Fabrics

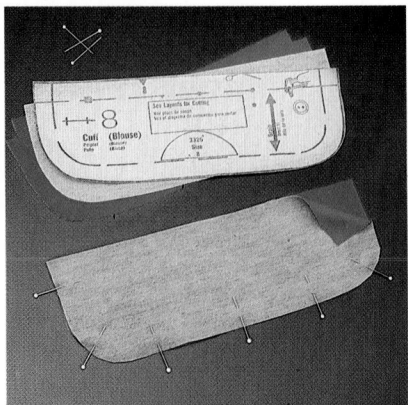

Cut interfacing the same size and shape as garment section. Do not trim seam allowances from edges of fusible interfacings.

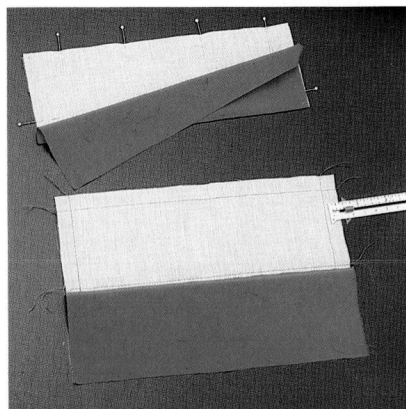

Machine-baste sew-in interfacing just beyond seamline. Use loose stitch. Sew beyond ends to prevent distortion; do not backstitch.

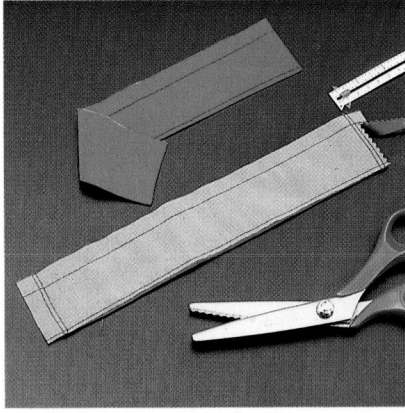

Trim enclosed seam allowances to ¼" (6 mm) or less, using pinking shears to prevent ridges. It is not necessary to grade these seams.

Marking & Stitching

To transfer pattern markings, try the quick methods using a tracing wheel or liquid marker. Both make temporary stitching guidelines that will not harm or show through fine fabrics. Because these methods yield marks that last briefly, keep pattern pieces pinned to fabric sections until it is time to sew; then transfer markings.

Stitching Tips

Upper tension adjustments can correct an unbalanced stitch. It may be necessary to reduce the upper tension.

Skipped stitches are a common problem. To prevent them, prewash the fabric and stitch slowly, using the straight-stitch throat plate and presser foot. Change the needle often, and use a fine thread.

Even Feed™ foot keeps fabric layers from shifting during stitching. This foot draws thin, lightweight fabrics evenly under the needle as you stitch.

New needle may prevent puckering and snagging of fabric. Some fabrics dull needle tips quickly, and this affects stitch quality.

Straight-stitch throat plate helps prevent fabric from being pulled into the opening. Or when using the zigzag plate, cover the opening with strapping tape, and pierce the tape with a needle; clean adhesive residue from needle with alcohol.

Straight-stitch presser foot is best for straight stitching. This foot has a flat surface for better stitching. Do not use the special-purpose foot, which has grooves or a shaped bottom surface.

Mark with tracing wheel or liquid marker. When using tracing wheel, work on hard surface and apply firm pressure to mark fabric with creases. Do not use tracing paper. Use smooth-edged wheel, and cover pattern with thin plastic, such as a food storage bag. When using liquid marker, insert superfine pins through pattern and fabric into cutting surface. Lift top fabric layer to mark both layers with dots where pins enter fabric. Use pen with disappearing ink.

Preventing Puckered Stitches

Place needle in fabric at start of seam; then lower presser foot. To prevent thread jams at start of stitching, hold thread ends in one hand while guiding fabric with the other hand.

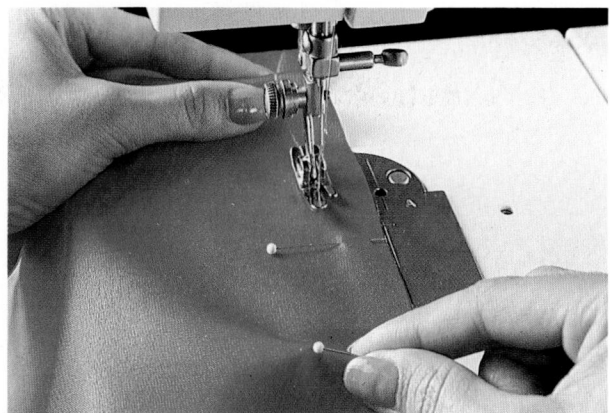

Practice taut sewing. Place one hand behind needle and one hand in front to keep fabric smooth. Hold fabric firmly as you sew, so stitches lie flat when seam is relaxed. Do not *pull* fabric through machine. This causes uneven stitches and broken needles.

Seams

There are several methods for making neat, narrow seams on fine fabrics. Make a variety of seams on fabric scraps to decide which method pleases you the most. Also, within a single garment you may want to use more than one style of seam, changing sewing methods according to the seam shape or location.

French seam can be made on a conventional sewing machine (**1**) or an overlock machine (**2**). Because all raw edges are enclosed, this seam is especially good for sheer and silky fabrics that ravel. French seams will not stretch, so they are most suitable for straight seams and seams that need to be stabilized. Do not use French seams where the fabric is cut on the bias grain, such as armholes, kimono and raglan underarms, and curved princess seams.

How to Sew a French Seam

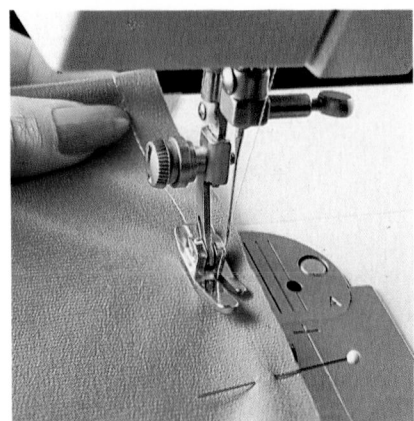

1) Stitch *wrong* sides together, using ⅜" (1 cm) seam allowance. Use short straight stitches.

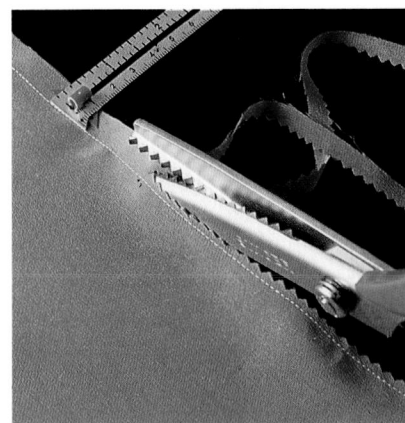

2) Trim seam to ⅛" (3 mm). Use pinking shears so no stray fibers show on right side of seam.

3) Fold fabric with right sides together, press seam edge, and stitch ¼" (6 mm) seam. Press finished seam to one side.

5   6   7   8

Hairline seam for enclosed seams in areas such as collars, cuffs, and facings is nearly invisible. It can be made on an overlock machine (**3**) or with narrow zigzag stitches (**4**).

Overlocked seam, made on a three-thread (**5**) or four-thread (**6**) overlock machine is used on most ready-to-wear garments. Overlock machines easily handle thin, slippery fabrics without puckers or

other stitching problems. Seams are stitched and trimmed in one operation.

Double-stitched seam is a traditional plain seam variation that is effective on fabrics that do not ravel easily. Use a short straight stitch (**7**) or three-step zigzag stitch (**8**) for the second stitching. Trim seam allowance close to second stitching.

How to Sew a French Seam with an Overlock Machine

1) Stitch ⅜" (1 cm) from raw edges, *wrong* sides together. Use overlock machine with cutting blades engaged to trim seams slightly wider than ⅛" (3 mm).

2) Fold fabric with right sides together. Press seam edge lightly with tip of iron.

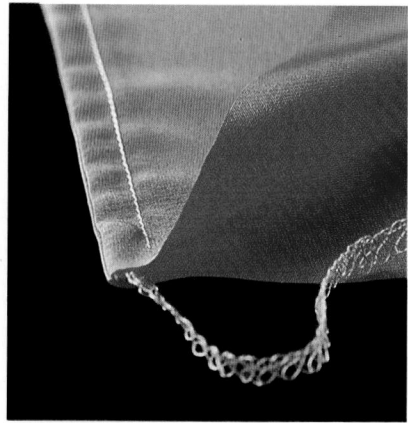

3) Stitch on seamline, ¼" (6 mm) from edge, using conventional machine straight stitch.

How to Sew an Enclosed Zigzag Hairline Seam

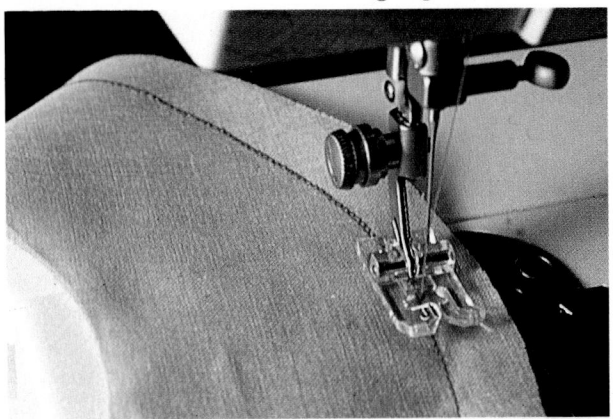

1) Stitch ⅝" (1.5 cm) seam with right sides together, using 12 to 16 stitches per inch (2.5 cm). Then stitch the seam again with a narrow zigzag, positioning work so needle pierces fabric next to original seam.

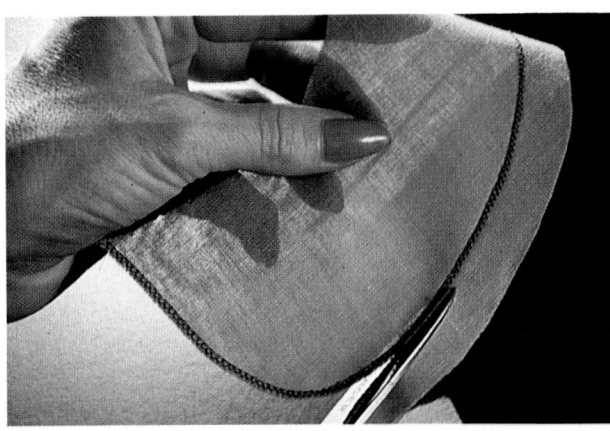

2) Trim seam allowances close to zigzag stitches. Use small, sharp scissors for clean, neat edge. Turn right side out and press with tip of iron to prevent seam imprint on right side.

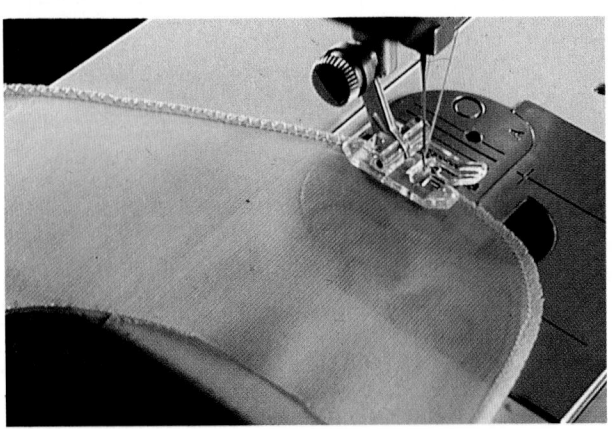

Alternative method. Stitch ⅝" (1.5 cm) seam with right sides together. Trim seam allowance to scant ⅛" (3 mm). Using narrow zigzag, stitch so needle pierces seamline and overcasts raw edge. Stitch with the grain to avoid creating a fringe. Adjust tension to prevent puckering.

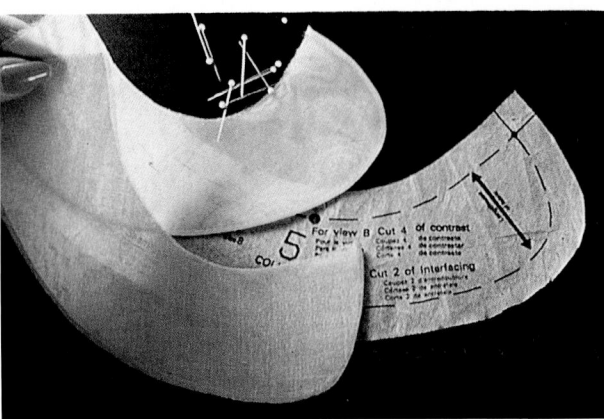

Finished enclosed hairline seam used on collars and cuffs is barely visible, even on the sheerest of fabrics.

How to Sew an Enclosed Overlocked Hairline Seam

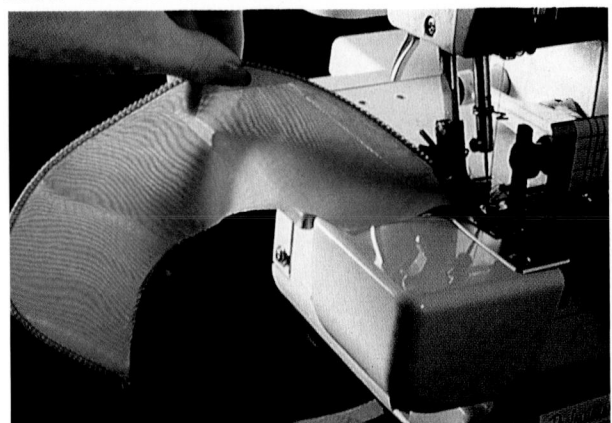

1) Stitch ⅝" (1.5 cm) seam with right sides together, setting overlock machine for short, narrow stitch. Tighten all tensions when using fine thread.

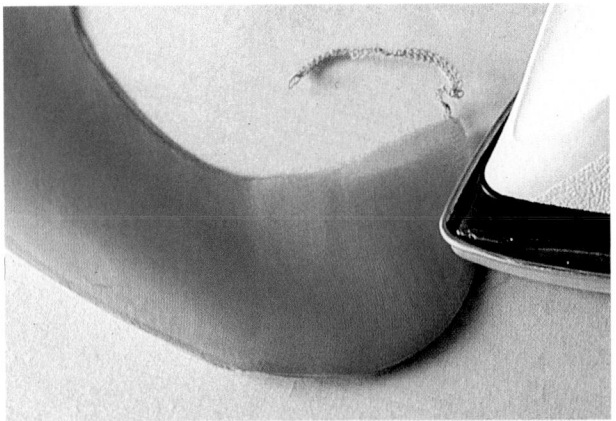

2) Turn garment section right side out. Fold edge along overlocked seam. Press edge with tip of iron to prevent seam imprint on right side.

Bindings & Underlinings

Facings that show through to the right side detract from the beauty of a sheer garment. Omit facings on sheers and finish the garment edges with a narrow French binding (above). All raw edges are completely concealed in the folds of the bias strip for a neat look. For a faster finish, bind the raw edge with purchased sheer tricot bias strips, and topstitch. Underline selected garment sections with self-fabric or a lightweight lining fabric. An underlining makes a sheer fabric opaque and helps to conceal facings and other construction details. When only portions of a transparently sheer garment are underlined, choose an underlining to match your skin tones; the entire garment will look more uniform in color.

The Hong Kong underlining method has the added benefit of self-finishing some of the raw edges. Some garment sections may be underlined this way. For example, if making a dress, use a Hong Kong underlining for the major front and back bodice sections only. Make the sleeves from a single layer of fabric to emphasize the sheer effect. Use a separate

slip lining in the skirt so the sheer outer layer seems to float on top. The neckline, armhole, and front or back closure facings on the bodice can be bound or sewn with traditional facings and will not show through the garment.

On silky fabrics, facings present different problems. Most facing edges must be finished without added bulk because even a single line of stitching can show through as an imprint on the outside of the garment. If the fabric selvage is even and free of puckers after preshrinking, use it as a finished facing edge. Position the facing pattern for layout so the selvage falls on the cutting line. This method works only for facings with a straight outer edge.

On opaque silky fabrics, fuse interfacing up to the edge of the facings. It is sufficient to finish the free edge of the facing by trimming with pinking shears. Press lightly. If the front or back faced edge is straight, omit facing seams by cutting the facing all in one with the body section.

How to Finish an Edge with French Binding

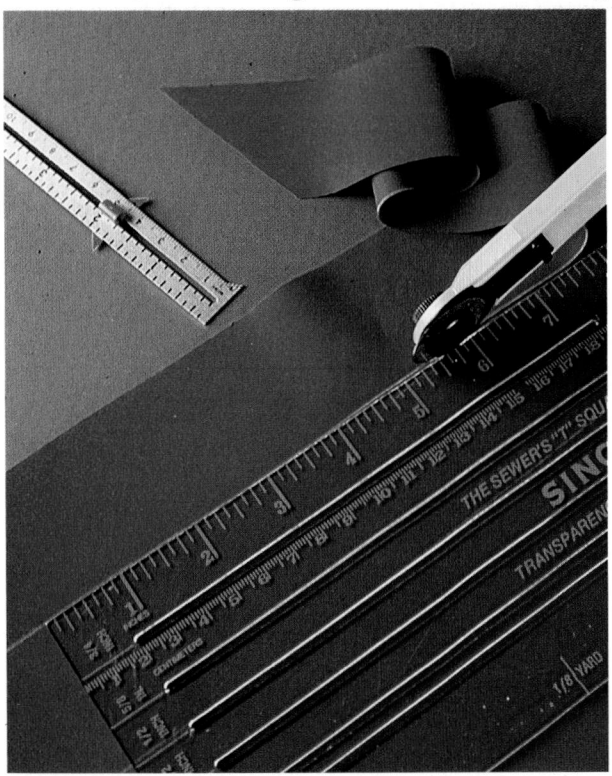

1) Cut bias strip seven times desired finished width of binding. For ¼" (6 mm) binding, cut strip 1¾" (4.5 cm) wide.

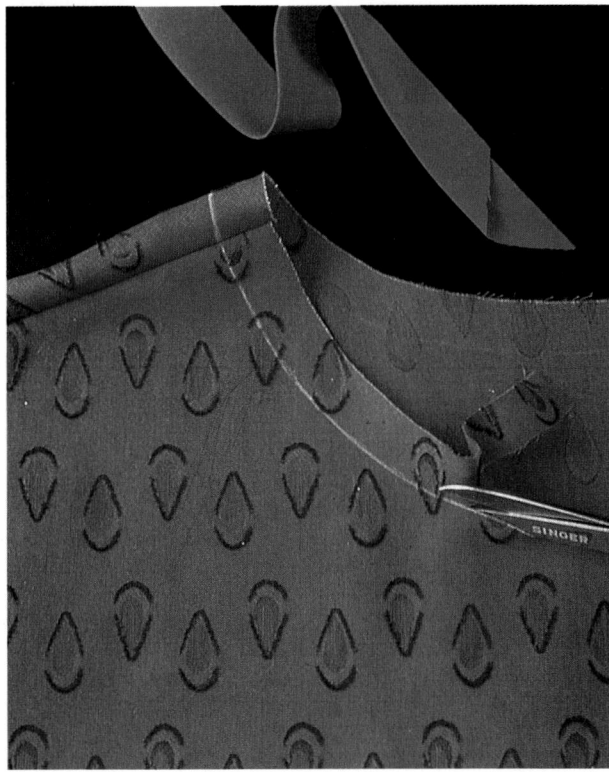

2) Fold bias strip in half lengthwise with wrong sides together; press. Mark seamline on garment edge; then trim off entire seam allowance.

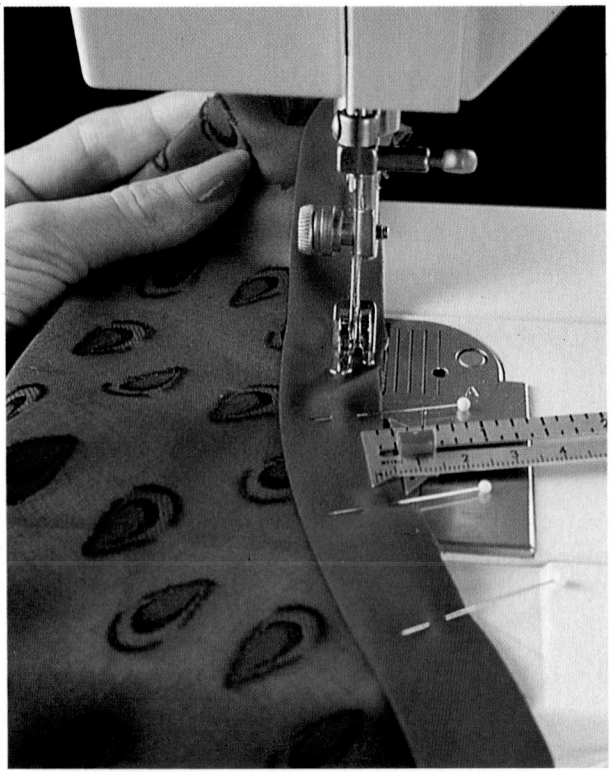

3) Stitch binding to outside of garment, matching all raw edges. Use seam allowance equal to desired finished width of binding.

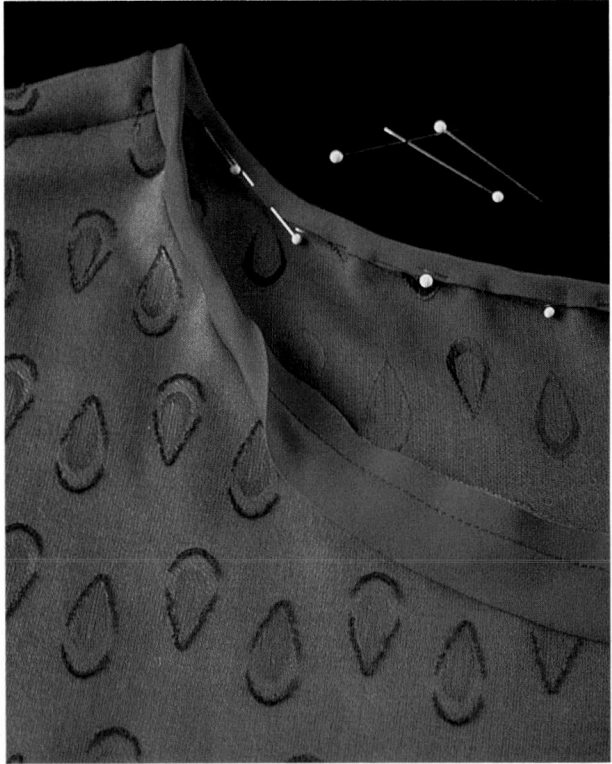

4) Fold binding over raw edges to inside of garment. Press lightly. Secure free edge of binding with one of three techniques shown opposite.

Techniques for Finishing a French Binding

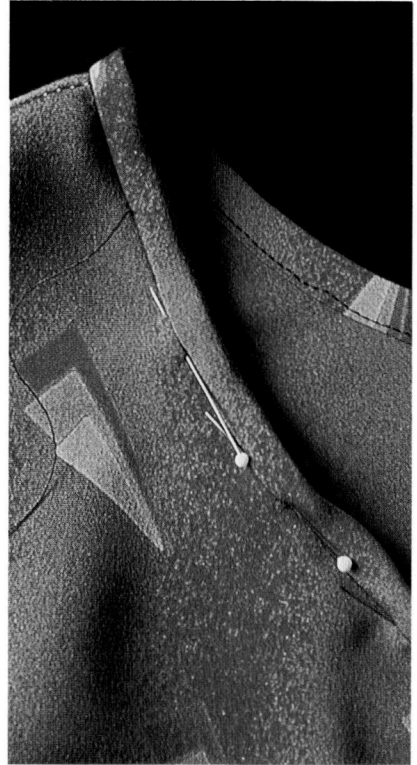

Stitch in the ditch. Working from right side of garment, stitch in the ditch formed by binding seam.

Topstitching. Working from right side of garment, topstitch close to seam edge of binding.

Slipstitching. Working from wrong side of garment, slipstitch binding fold by hand to binding seam.

How to Finish an Edge with Tricot Binding or Self-fabric Binding

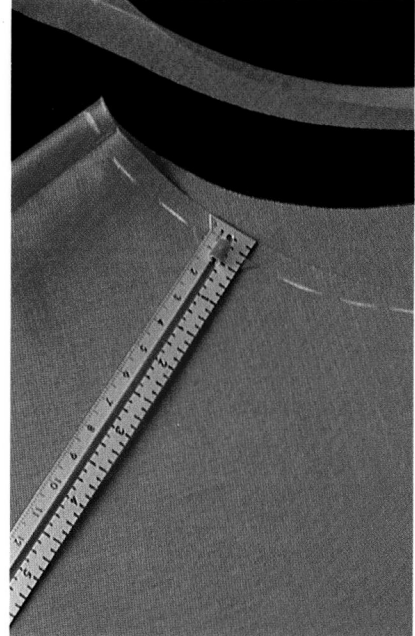

1) Fold 1¼" (3.2 cm) wide binding in half lengthwise, wrong sides together. Press lightly. Trim garment seam allowance to ¼" (6 mm). Stitch binding to right side, raw edges even.

2) Fold binding to inside of the garment so binding does not show on right side. Press lightly with tip of iron.

3) Edgestitch binding ⅛" (3 mm) from edge, working from right side of garment.

How to Sew a Hong Kong Underlining

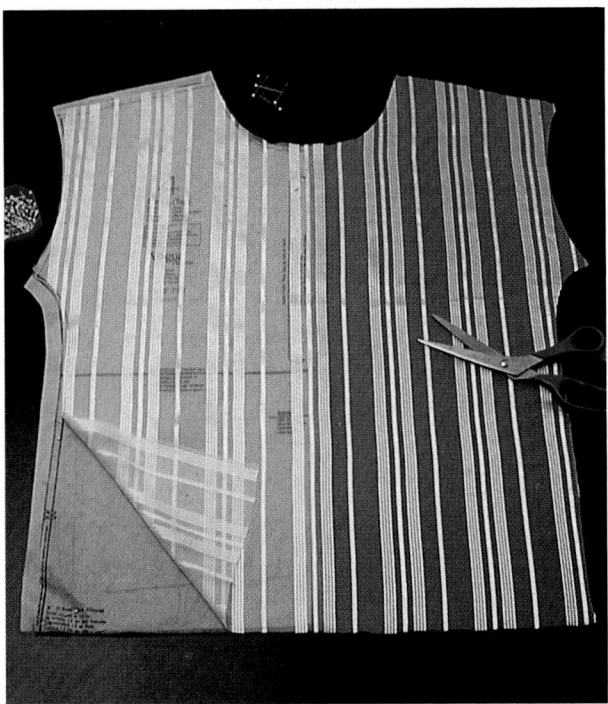

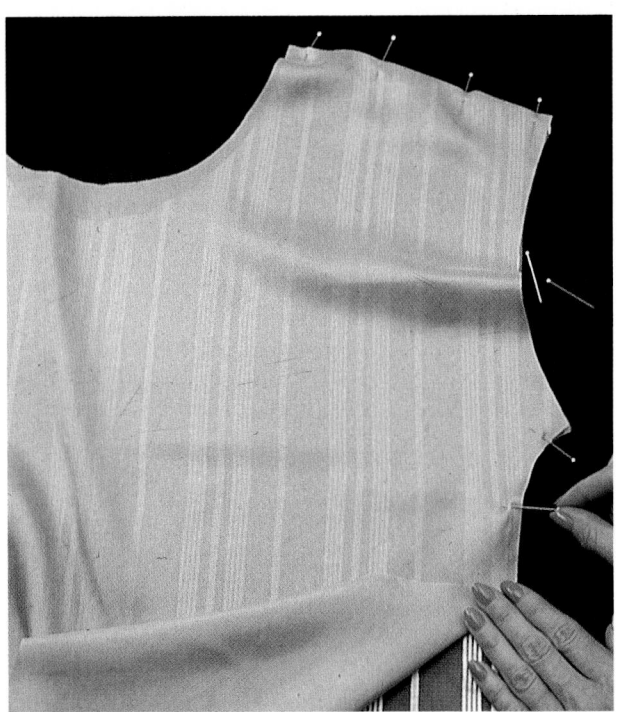

1) Cut garment sections from pattern with regular ⅝" (1.5 cm) seam allowances. To cut underlining, use main front and back pattern pieces. Add ½" (1.3 cm) to all straight seam allowances, such as side, center front, center back, and shoulder seams. Total adjusted seam allowance is 1⅛" (2.8 cm).

2) Pin fabric to underlining, with right sides together, at vertical seams and shoulder seams. Match raw edges of both fabric layers.

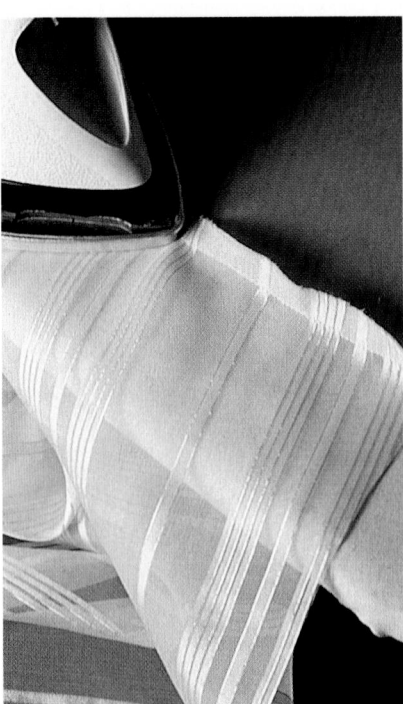

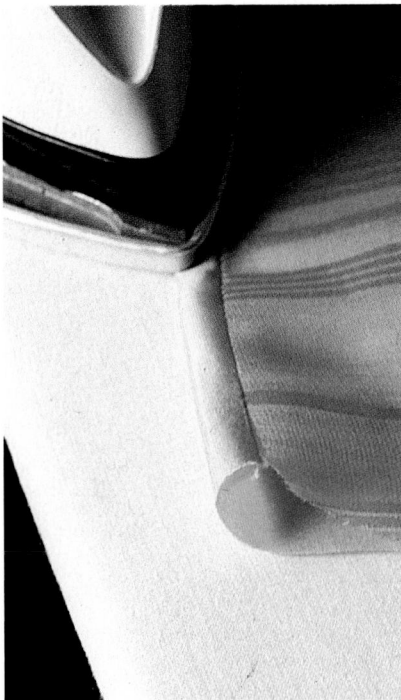

3) Stitch fabric to underlining with ¼" (6 mm) seams on edges pinned in step 2. Armhole, neckline, and lower edges are left open. Press seams toward underlining.

4) Turn right side out through one open edge. Press underlining so it wraps evenly over fabric seams. Outer fabric remains flat.

5) Stitch regular ⅝" (1.5 cm) seam to join sections. Press seam open. Underlining wraps over edge of seam allowance to finish edges.

Set-in Sleeves

Some silky fabrics, especially those made from polyester fibers, do not ease smoothly. This quality can present problems at the cap of a set-in sleeve, where extra fabric must be eased to fit the armhole seam. The ordinary sewing method, using two rows of easestitching to reduce the size of the sleeve cap, often creates small pleats or puckers instead of a smoothly rounded cap. Also, on some silks the ease-stitching may leave marks when stitching is removed.

Prevent both problems by using a strip of sheer tricot bias binding to preshape sleeve caps. The

binding remains in place after the sleeve is set in. One edge of the binding acts as a sleeve head, supporting the eased seam allowance so it lies smooth without ripples. The other edge wraps over the trimmed seam allowances for a neat finish.

In addition, some synthetic silks may not ease smoothly unless you remove some of the extra fabric in the sleeve cap. The easiest way to do this is to use a slightly deeper seam allowance on the sleeve only. Taper back into the original seam allowance at the seam notches, front and back.

How to Ease a Set-in Sleeve with Tricot Binding

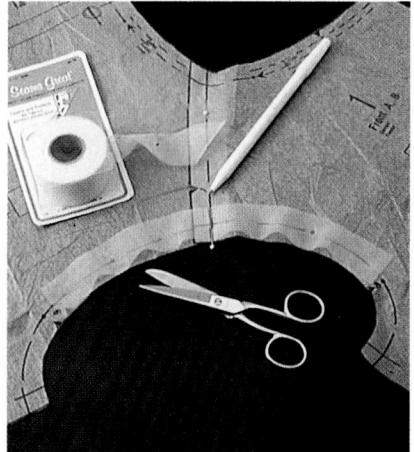

1) Cut 1¼" (3.2 cm) wide sheer tricot bias binding long enough to fit from front to back notches of armhole seam. Mark shoulder seam location on tricot strip. Pin tricot binding to wrong side of sleeve cap, even with raw edge.

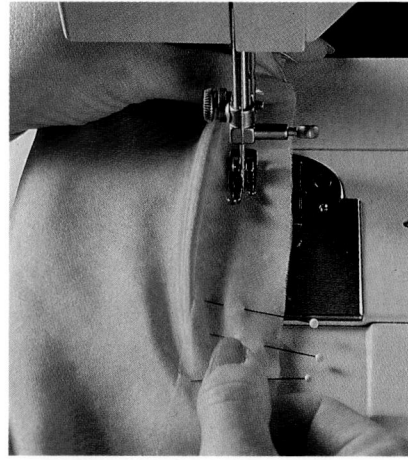

2) Stitch binding to sleeve cap, just inside seamline, stretching binding to fit. Use 10 to 12 stitches per inch (2.5 cm). Relax binding as you stitch 1" (2.5 cm) over top of sleeve cap. Press lightly with tip of iron on seamline to shrink in ease.

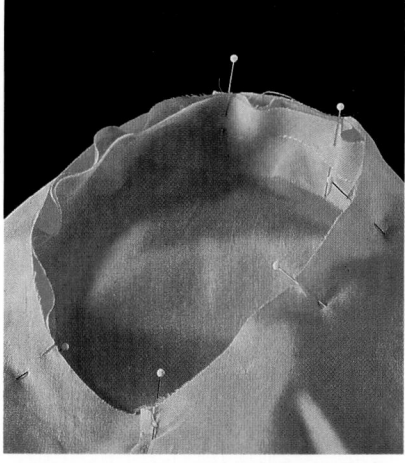

3) Pin sleeve into armhole. To ease further, gently pull up bobbin thread. To ease less, snip several stitches and stretch binding slightly as you stitch. Stitch sleeve to garment, binding side up.

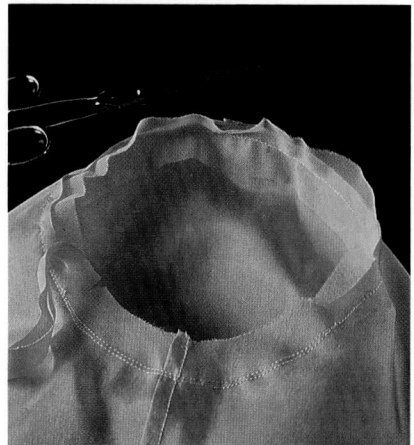

4) Trim armhole seam allowance to ¼" (6 mm). Do not trim tricot binding. Wrap binding over raw edge of trimmed seam allowance.

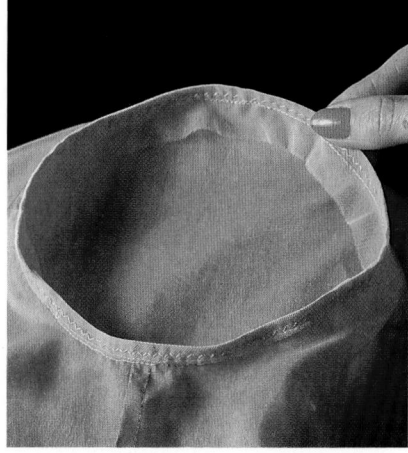

5) Stitch tricot binding to armhole seam allowance. Use additional strip of tricot binding or 3-step zigzag stitch to finish underarm seam between notches.

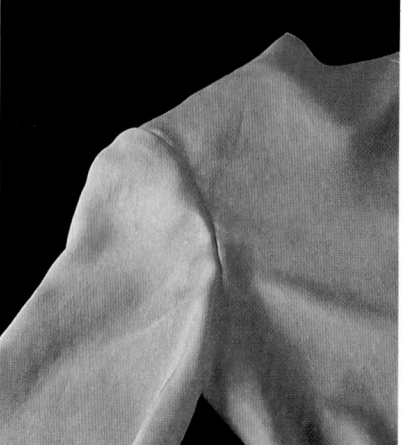

6) Turn sleeve to right side. Sleeve should be smoothly rounded with no puckers on the seamline. Tricot binding acts as sleeve head to support sleeve cap.

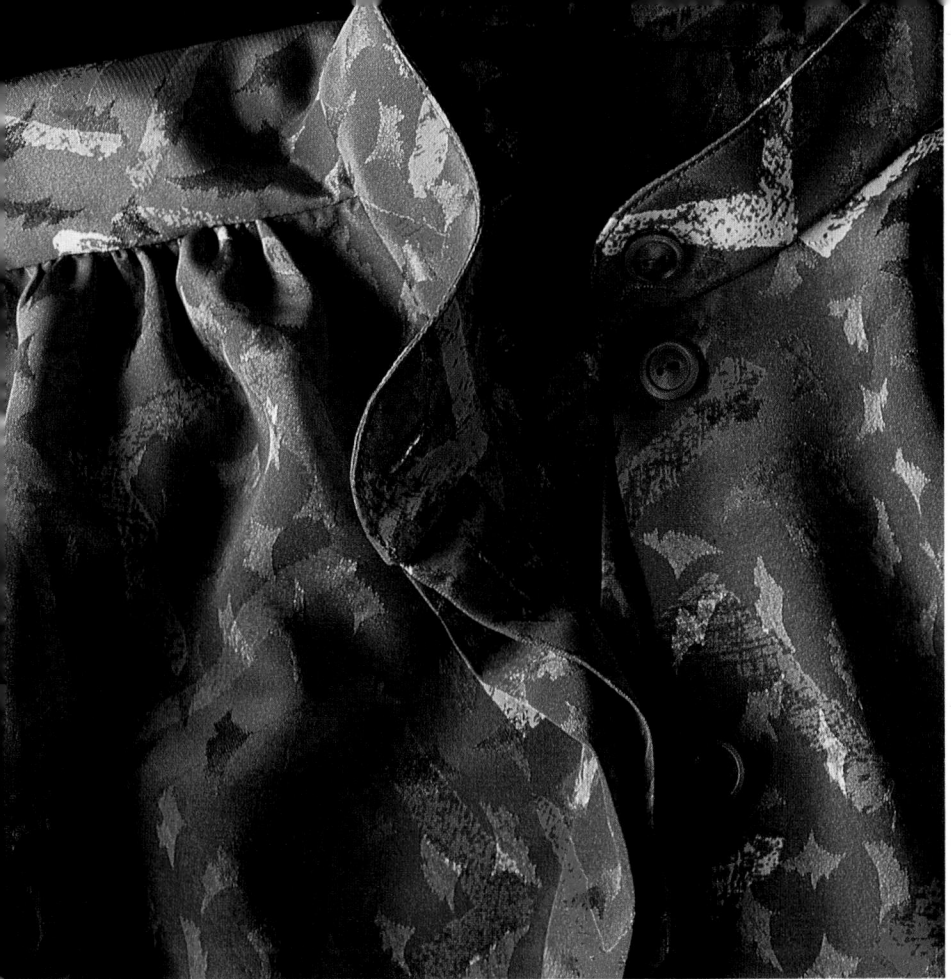

Hidden Plackets

On dresses or blouses with front or back buttoned closings, you can make a hidden placket to eliminate the facings. This method uses a cut-in-one bodice extension as both the facing and interfacing, so it is a shortcut as well as a solution to the problem of a facing showing through in sheers. This facing finish is also appropriate to use on any of the lightweight silky fabrics.

Make a sample buttonhole when working with sheer and silky fabrics. Adjustments in stitch length and width, as well as a reduction in needle tension, may be needed before your machine can make a fine buttonhole on these fabrics. A new needle is always a good idea to prevent snags and pulls.

How to Sew a Hidden Placket

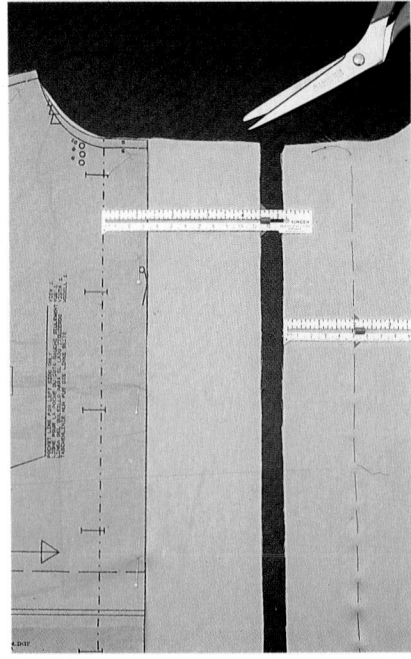

1) Extend bodice front pattern 4½" (11.5 cm) from center front mark to cut right-hand side. Extend bodice front pattern 2½" (6.5 cm) from center front mark to cut left-hand side.

2) Fold under 4" (10 cm) on right-hand bodice. Press first crease. Open up folded fabric, and turn raw edge under to meet crease; press second crease. Do not open up folded fabric.

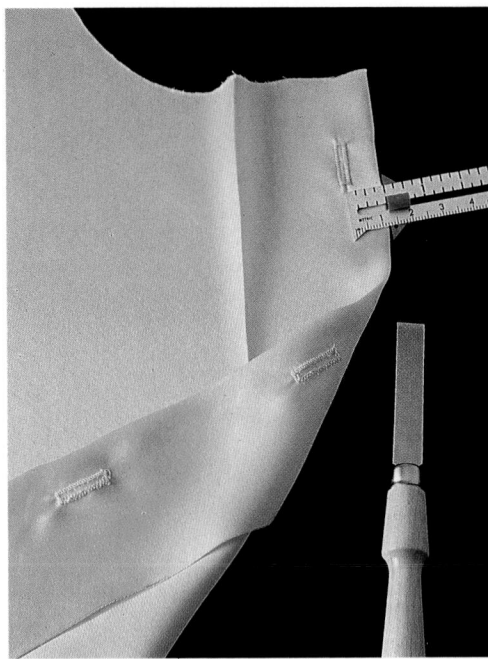

3) Make buttonholes (opposite) ½" (1.3 cm) from edge, stitching buttonholes through both layers of fabric to form flap. Work with bodice section right side up. Position buttonholes parallel to edge.

Tips for Making Buttonholes

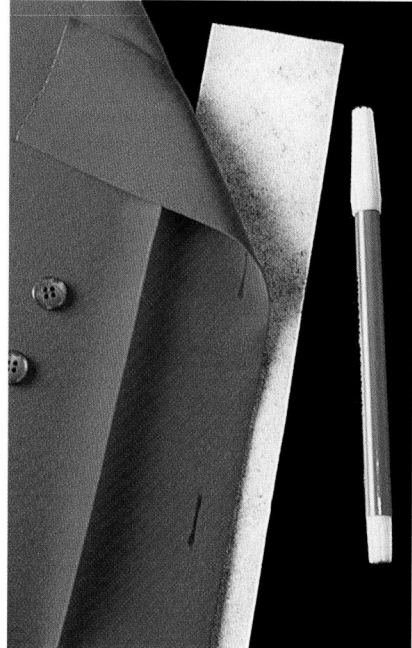

Back buttonhole area with nonwoven tear-away stabilizer before stitching. This prevents fabric from stretching and keeps buttonholes free of puckers.

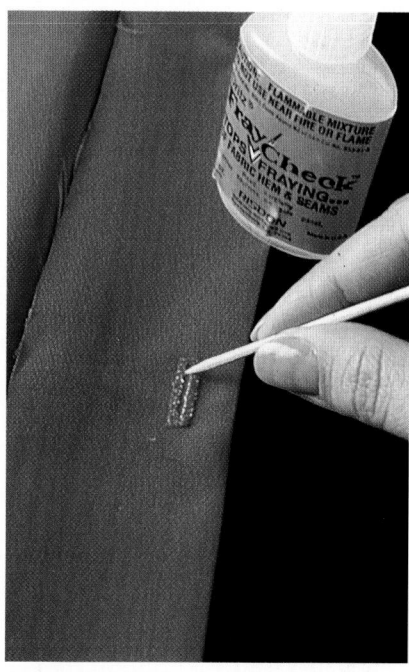

Apply liquid fray preventer (with a toothpick or fine art brush) to fabric at center of buttonhole. Do this inside garment, before cutting buttonhole open. Dry completely.

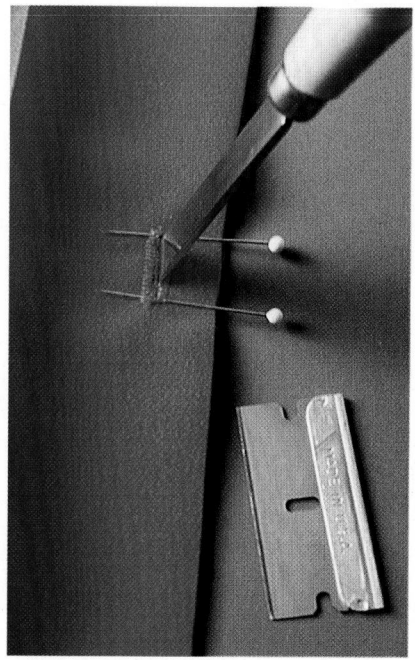

Slit buttonhole open with chisel buttonhole cutting tool to avoid snags and frayed threads. Single-edged razor blade or hobby knife can also be used. Place straight pins at end of buttonhole to prevent cutting into stitches.

4) Turn flap under on first crease, forming placket with three fabric layers. Topstitch 1" (2.5 cm) from placket edge. Press flat, as sewn, to embed stitches.

5) Fold buttonhole flap toward center front. Press from wrong side. Free edge of buttonhole flap lies on top of placket edge.

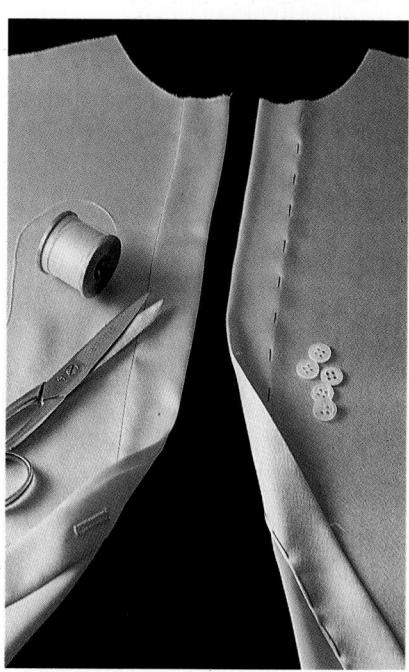

6) Fold under 2" (5 cm) on left-hand bodice, and press crease. Open up fabric to bring raw edge to meet crease. Press second crease. Fold on first crease; hand-baste. Sew buttons through all three fabric layers. Buttons hold layers in place.

Narrow Hems

On sheer fabrics narrow hems look best because there is minimal show-through to the outside of a garment. The regular 2" to 2½" (5 to 6.5 cm) hem **(1)** as specified in the pattern can be used on silky fabrics. Apply with loose catchstitch or blindstitch.

Some silky fabrics may look better with narrow hems, because wide hems may be too heavy and can interfere with the way the garment drapes. Narrow hems are also used on ruffles and ties. There are three easy methods for making narrow hems: overlocking the raw edge **(2)**, making a rolled hem on an overlock machine **(3)**, and enclosing the raw edge with sheer tricot bias binding **(4)**. The overlocked edge and tricot-bound hem should be used only on tuck-in shirts and blouses, where the finished edge is hidden. A rolled overlocked hem can be used almost anywhere.

Other methods for making narrow hems require some practice, but once mastered, the work goes quickly. A topstitched hem **(5)** is practical for fabrics that ravel, but two lines of machine stitches show on the right side, so it is quite visible. A hairline hem **(6)**, made with a combination of straight and zigzag stitches, is practically invisible. Use the narrow hemming-foot hem **(7)** to eliminate excessive stitching and pressing. A hand-rolled hem **(8)**, although the most time-consuming, is an elegant couture finish.

1   2   3   4   5

Easy Narrow Hems

  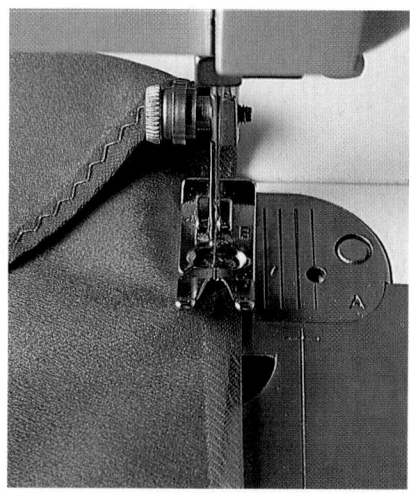

Overlocked edge. Use three-thread overlock machine to finish raw edge instead of sewing traditional hem. Position garment for overlocking so cutting blades of machine trim fabric on finished hemline as you stitch.

Rolled overlocked hem. Adjust three-thread overlock machine to make rolled hem. Position garment so hem allowance is trimmed off by cutting blades.

Tricot-bound hem. Trim garment on hemline; use ⅝" (1.5 cm) wide sheer tricot bias binding to encase raw edge. Stretch binding slightly so it cups over raw edge. Use zigzag or straight stitch.

6   7   8

How to Sew a Hairline Hem

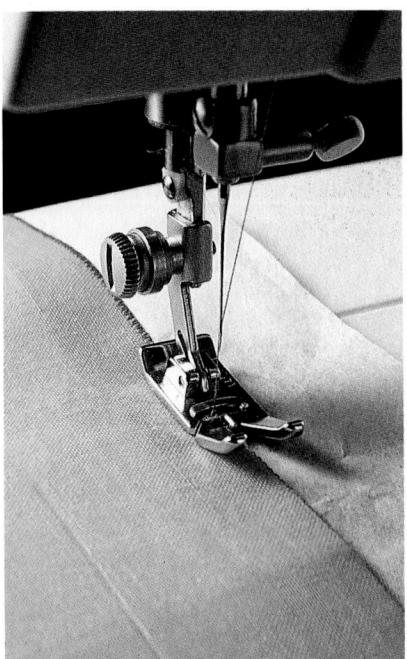

1) Stay-stitch on garment hemline. Use short straight stitch, 12 to 16 per inch (2.5 cm). Use taut sewing to prevent puckered stitches on thin fabrics. Fold hem under on stitching line. Press.

2) Zigzag with short, narrow stitches over hem edge, working from right side of garment. Stitch over tear-away or tissue paper to stabilize fabric and to prevent it from being pulled into throat plate.

3) Tear away the paper and discard. Use small, sharp scissors to trim hem allowance close to stitches, taking care not to cut into garment or stitches.

How to Sew a Narrow Topstitched Hem

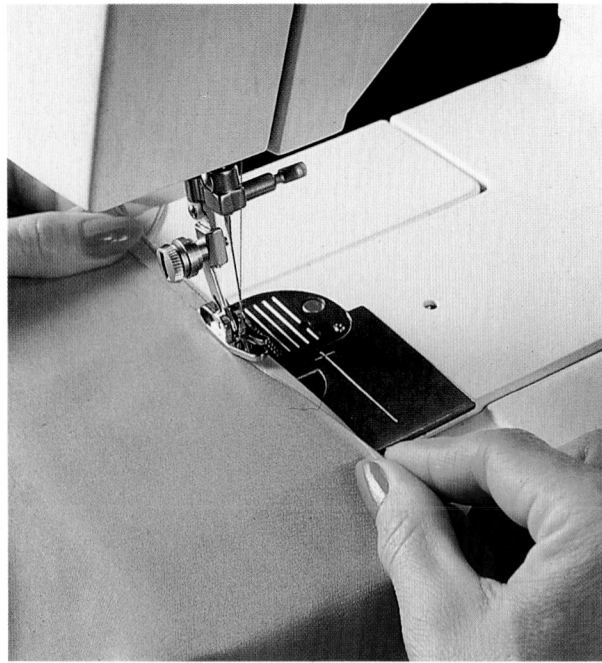

1) Fold under ¼" (6 mm), and edgestitch fold. Working from wrong side of fabric, use fingers to hold fabric in position. Use short straight stitch, 12 to 16 per inch (2.5 cm).

2) Fold under ¼" to ½" (6 mm to 1.3 cm). On slippery fabrics, wider ⅜" to ½" (1 to 1.3 cm) hem is easier to handle than ¼" (6 mm) hem. Press. Edgestitch both folds of hem.

How to Sew a Hand-rolled Hem

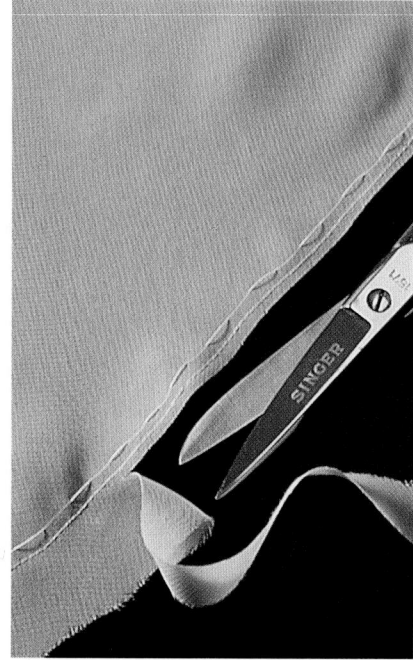

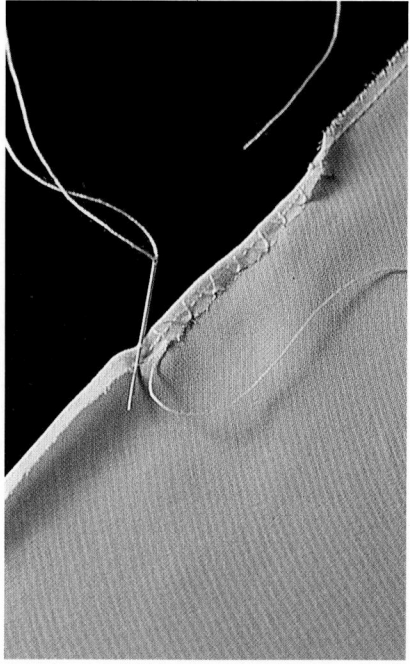

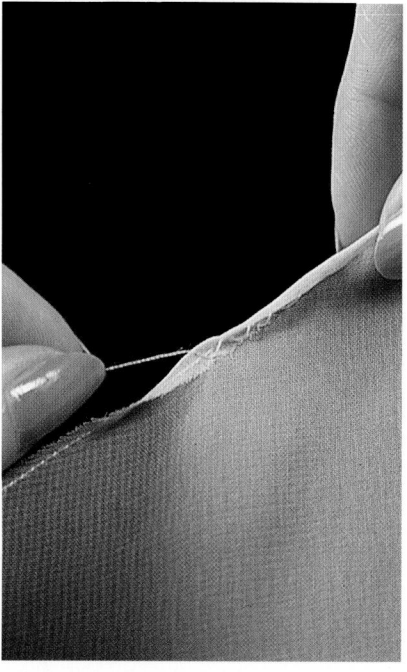

1) Stitch ⅛" (3 mm) below the marking for hem, using short stitch. Trim off hem allowance a scant ⅛" (3 mm) below stitching line. Press.

2) Fold edge to wrong side, just above stitching line. With fine needle and thread, take a stitch through the fold, then ⅛" (3 mm) from fold, catching a single thread. Continue alternating stitches, working from right to left.

3) Pull the thread to draw fold down and form hem after making about 6 stitches.

How to Sew a Narrow Hem with a Hemmer Foot

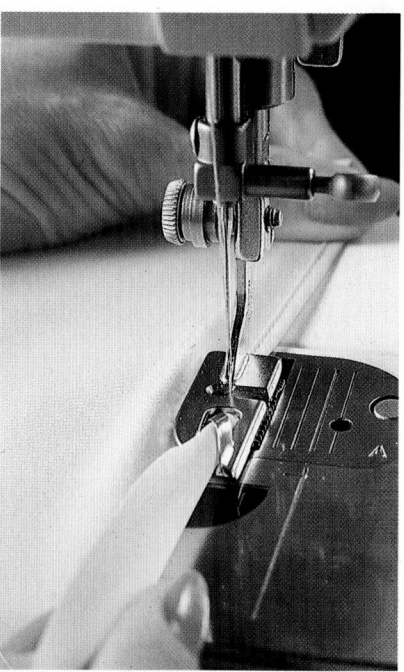

1) Fold under a double ⅛" (3 mm) hem, and crease it for about 2" (5 cm). Place the hem under the foot, and stitch through creased fold for several stitches.

2) Leave needle down. Raise presser foot. Hold thread ends in left hand, and with right hand evenly guide raw edge in front of hemmer into scroll.

3) Guide fold of fabric through scroll, holding fabric taut behind hemmer. As you sew, keep same width of fabric in scroll at all times.

Special Occasion Fabrics

Lace & Embroidered Fabrics

Laces look fragile and delicate but are actually easy to sew. True laces have a net or mesh background, which has no grainline and does not ravel. You can cut into the fabric freely for creative pattern layouts, seams need no time-consuming edge finishes, and hemming requires little more than trimming close to the edges of prominent motifs.

The openwork designs of lace fabrics have rich histories. Some laces still bear the names of the European localities where they were once made by hand from silk, cotton, or linen fibers. Today, many laces are made by machine from easy-care cotton blends, polyester, acrylic, or nylon.

1) Alençon lace has filled-in motifs outlined by soft satin cord on a sheer net background. One or both lengthwise edges usually have a finished border.

2) Chantilly lace has delicate floral motifs worked on a fine net background and outlined with silky threads. A popular bridal fabric, Chantilly lace usually has an allover pattern.

3) Eyelet is a finely woven cotton or polyester/cotton fabric embroidered with a satin-stitched openwork design. Even though eyelet embroideries are not true laces, they require pattern layout and pressing techniques similar to those for laces.

4) Peau d'ange is a form of Chantilly lace made with a flossy yarn to give it a soft texture.

5) Venice lace is made from heavy yarns and unique stitches that give it a three-dimensional texture. Picot bridges join the motifs. Venice lace does not have the net background that is typical of most laces.

6) Point d'esprit has an open net or fine tulle background with a pattern of embroidered dots.

7) Cluny lace is made from heavy cotton-like yarns and looks hand-crocheted. It usually has paddle or wheel motifs and may have raised knots as part of the design.

8) Schiffli is an embroidered sheer or semi-sheer fabric decorated on a Schiffli machine, which imitates hand embroidery stitches.

Guide to Sewing Laces

Equipment & Techniques	Delicate Chantilly, peau d'ange, point d'esprit	Embroidered Eyelet, Schiffli	Textured Alençon, Cluny, Venice
Machine Needles	Size 8 (60) or 9 (65)	Size 9 (65) or 11 (75)	Size 11 (75)
Stitch Length	12 to 16 per inch (2.5 cm)	10 to 12 per inch (2.5 cm)	10 to 12 per inch (2.5 cm)
Millimeter Stitch Setting	2.5 to 2	3 to 2.5	3 to 2.5
Thread	Extra-fine	All-purpose	All-purpose
Hand Needles	Betweens, size 7 or 8	Betweens, size 7 or 8	Betweens, size 7 or 8
Interfacings	Omit	Omit	Omit
Special Seams	Lapped, overlocked, double-stitched	Overlocked, double-stitched	Lapped, double-stitched
Special Hems	Self-hem, appliquéd	Self-hem	Self-hem, appliquéd, horsehair braid

How Laces, Eyelets & Embroideries Are Sold

Fabric stores may stock a selection of laces and eyelets or special order them for you. *Imported laces* are among the most expensive and can have intricate, handworked details. Some imported laces are re-embroidered to emphasize the outline of prominent motifs, with the cords clipped by hand between motifs. Widths as narrow as 9" or 18" (23 or 46 cm) make imported laces more suitable for trims or selected portions of a garment than for an entire garment. *Domestic laces*, made by machine, are less intricate but more economical. Generous widths make them practical for entire garments.

1) Allover lace has two straight edges and motifs that repeat regularly throughout the entire fabric. An allover lace can be used for an entire garment, or individual motifs cut out and used as appliqués. The average width is 45" (115 cm); it is also available in 36" (91.5 cm) and 54" (137 cm) widths.

2) Galloon lace has two scalloped edges, which can be used as borders and finished hems. A versatile form of lace, galloon can be cut into appliqués, used like a flounce, or the borders positioned creatively on major garment sections. It can be narrow for trims or as wide as an allover lace.

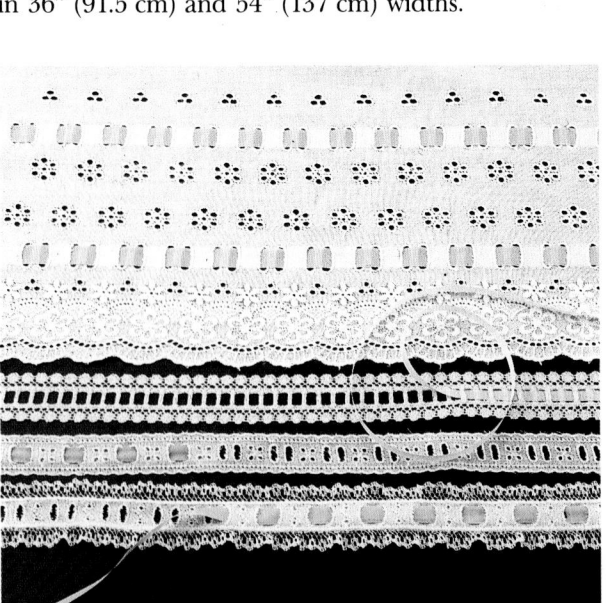

5) Beading has ladder-like openings through the center. Ribbon or another band trim can be woven through the openings. Beading can be used alone as a trim, combined with lace as an edging, or used as part of an allover design.

6) Edgings are trims with one scalloped edge. Narrower than flounces, widths range from ¼" to 6" (6 mm to 15 cm). Some edgings are pre-gathered with a sheer binding on the straight edge for use as ruffled trims.

The finest laces are made and sold in lengths called *strips*. These are pieces 4½ yds. to 6 yds. (4.15 to 5.50 m) long. You may buy the entire strip or just a portion of it. Threads remain along the edges of these laces where strips have been cut apart. Do not trim them off. They are a sign of quality lace and are left intact even on expensive designer garments.

Laces and eyelets are sold in several different forms. Some are meant for use as trims, some have finished borders, and others have multiple purposes. When you buy lace by the yard (meter), ask the salesperson to cut around a motif instead of straight across the fabric. You can then use the entire piece without wasting motifs that have been cut in half.

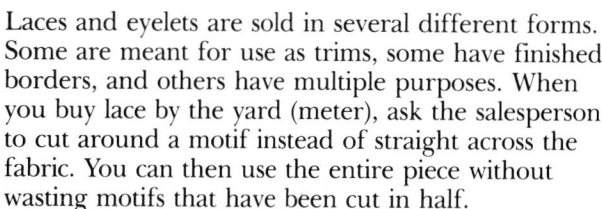

3) Flounce lace has one straight and one scalloped edge. Eyelet flounces have one unfinished edge. Wider than edgings, flounces are available in widths ranging from 6" to 36" (15 to 91.5 cm) for use as a flounce or ruffle on the lower edge or for garment sections such as yokes, sleeves, and bodices.

4) Appliqué lace is an isolated motif for use as a trim. Some appliqués come in right-hand and left-hand pairs to be used on collars or bodices.

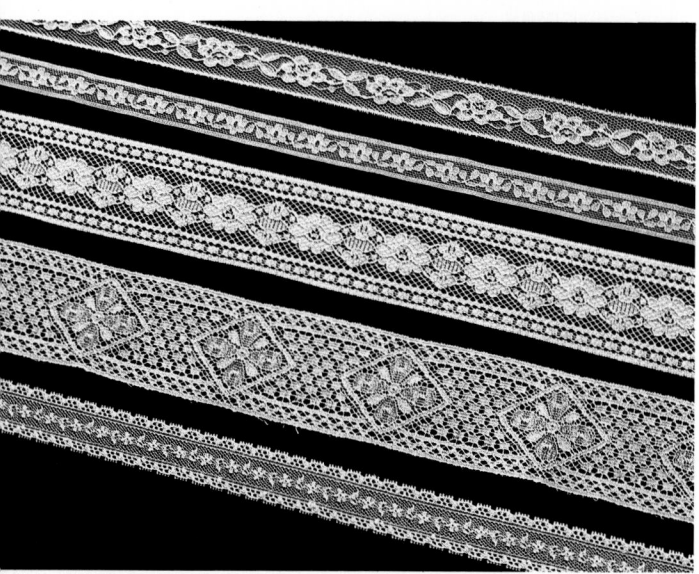

7) Insertions are trims with two straight edges. A lace insertion can be sewn between two seams or stitched on a fabric as a band trim. The trim width is usually ¼" to 6" (6 mm to 15 cm).

8) Sets are different forms and widths of lace with the same or coordinating motifs. A set may include a wide galloon, a narrow galloon, and an edging, each having the same pattern. A set can also consist of the same lace in plain and re-embroidered forms to be combined within a garment.

Techniques for Sewing Lace & Embroidered Fabrics

Select a pattern that suits the texture and weight of the lace fabric. Use heavy laces such as Alençon and Cluny for simple, fitted pattern silhouettes. Select lightweight laces, such as Chantilly, for patterns with full skirts and sleeves, and details such as ruffles.

Patterns for bridal and evening gowns that are illustrated in lace fabrics may require specific forms of lace, such as edgings of specific widths or a wide allover lace. Check the back of the pattern envelope to see if the lace fits the pattern requirements.

When considering a pattern that is not illustrated in laces, select a pattern with sections sized to fit the fabric width. If planning to use a bordered lace on sleeves, you may have to use a short-sleeved pattern if the lace is not wide enough for long sleeves, or place the lace at the lower edge of an organza sleeve. Facings, hems, and pockets are usually eliminated so you may need less fabric. Because lace has no grainline, it is possible to turn the pattern pieces to use an edge or border as a finished edge.

Fabric Preparation

Lace rarely requires any preparation for sewing. Most laces must be drycleaned. Although shrinkage is rare, if the care label on a lace fabric indicates it is washable, and you are combining it with other fabrics and trims to make a washable garment, then you should preshrink the lace. Add it to the other components of the garment as you preshrink them.

Facings, Interfacings & Underlinings

Facings and interfacings are not used on lace garments. Finish outer edges with lace trim, lace borders, or sheer tricot bias or French binding. Cut collars and cuffs as single layers, and finish the outer edges with lace trim or appliqué. Use a narrow seam to join them to the garment.

If you need to add body or support to lace, underline the lace with tulle netting. For example, you may choose to underline a fitted lace bodice or sleeves. The tulle netting adds strength without showing through or changing the character of the lace. A lining fabric in a contrasting color can also be used as an underlining. Although this makes the lace opaque, it shows off the lace design and hides seams, darts, and other details of inner construction.

Layout & Cutting

Pattern layout is an important preliminary step for lace fabrics. Begin by studying the details of the lace design. Unfold the fabric fully on the work surface, laying contrasting fabric underneath if necessary to make the design easier to read.

Note the placement of prominent motifs, the spacing of the repeats, and the depth of any borders. These affect pattern layout because the most noticeable motifs should be matched at the seams and centered or otherwise balanced on major garment sections, just like large fabric prints. If the design has one-way motifs, use a "with nap" pattern layout.

Plan at this point how to use the motifs creatively. Some laces have large primary motifs and smaller secondary motifs or borders that can be cut out and used as appliqués. To use borders as prefinished hems, determine the finished skirt and sleeve lengths before pattern layout. If you plan to trim the border from the fabric and sew it to the garment as a decorative edging, you do not need to determine lengths in advance so precisely.

Before cutting, decide which seam treatment you will be using. Allover laces can be sewn like sheer fabrics, with narrow seams. However, if you are working with a re-embroidered lace or a special heirloom lace with a large motif, lapped seams may be better. They will not interrupt the flow of the lace design around the garment because the seam is nearly invisible. With this method, pattern sections must be pinned in place and cut out one by one in sequence. You may use a combination of seams in one garment, with lapped seams at shoulder and side seams and narrow zigzag or double-stitched seams for set-in sleeves.

Once lace is cut, there is little margin for fitting changes. Fit the pattern before layout to avoid ripping out stitches later. Cut the pattern from lining or underlining fabric to use for fitting, as well as for the inside of the finished garment. Another method is to make a muslin trial garment. A third method is to make a full pattern from pattern tracing fabric and baste the sections together for a fitting. You can then use this pattern to cut out the lace.

Pressing

Avoid overhandling lace with pressing. If a light touch-up is needed, press with right side down on a well-padded surface to avoid flattening the lace texture. Use a press cloth to prevent the tip of the iron from catching or tearing the net background. If you are working with lace made from synthetic fibers, such as polyester or nylon, use a low temperature setting on the iron. Finger press seams, darts, and other construction details. Wear a thimble and press firmly. If further pressing is necessary, steam lightly, then finger press.

Layout for Lace Fabrics

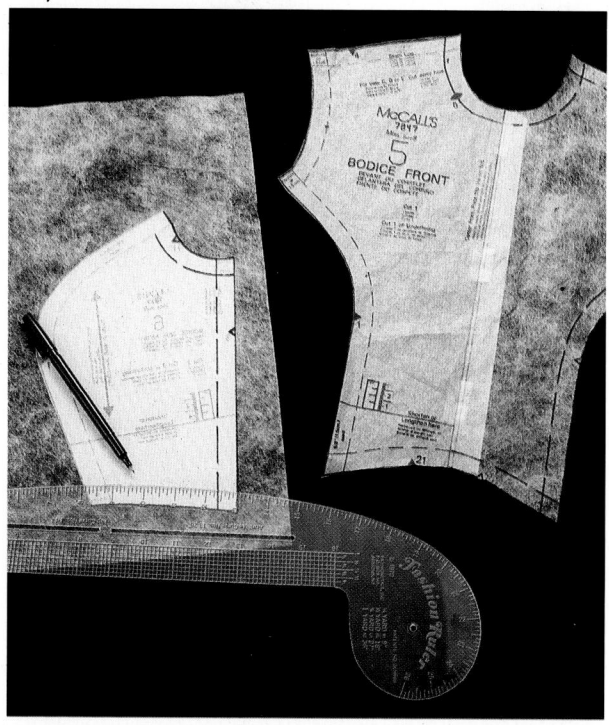

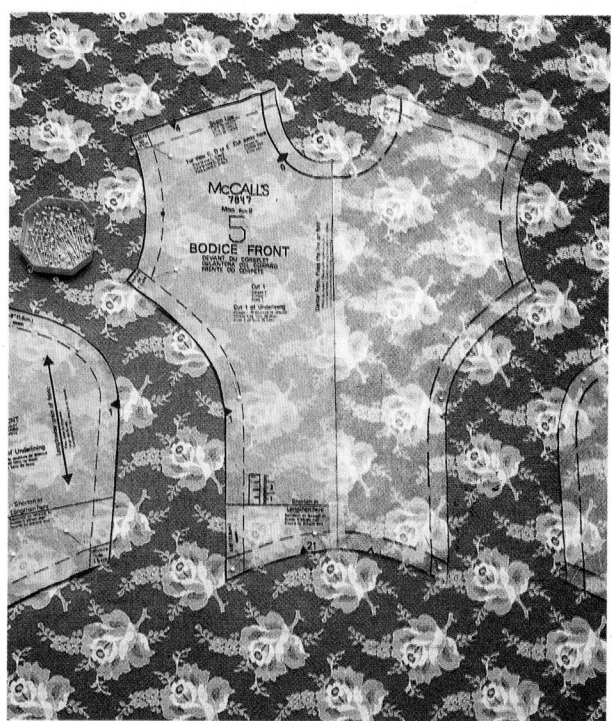

Draw full pattern pieces for all lace garment sections. Use transparent fabric, such as pattern tracing fabric or sheer nonwoven interfacing. Cut right and left sleeves by flipping tissue pattern over for second sleeve. Omit facings.

Lay out pattern on single layer of lace. Balance motifs right to left and top to bottom on major garment sections. Center important motifs above bustline on bodice front, and match motifs at seams. Use long pins to hold pattern on fabric; short pins may fall through open laces.

Study pattern piece and lace design to see if lace borders or prominent motifs can be positioned on straight edges of garment, such as necklines, yokes, sleeve hems, and skirt hems. Clip scalloped borders to appliqué on curved edges. Place inner points of lace scallops on pattern *seamlines* when using scallops for necklines or yoke edges. Place inner points on *hemline* for hem and sleeve edges.

Seams

Like seams on other see-through fabrics, seams on lace should be narrow and inconspicuous. A double-stitched seam (left) is made either with two rows of straight stitches ⅛" (3 mm) apart or with a combination of straight and zigzag stitching. A French seam is narrow with all raw edges enclosed (pages 26 and 27); it can be used on straight seams. An overlocked seam is also suitable for laces.

A lapped seam is a special way to handle lace. Stitched to follow the outline of the lace motifs, a lapped seam is practically invisible on the finished garment. To use this method, you must plan ahead and prepare the lapping seam allowances during pattern layout.

Stitch slowly, especially on open laces, so the toes of the presser foot do not snag the lace. To prevent snagging, cover the toes of the presser foot with transparent tape. Tissue paper under the lace prevents the lace from being pulled down through the hole in the zigzag throat plate.

How to Cut and Sew a Lapped Seam

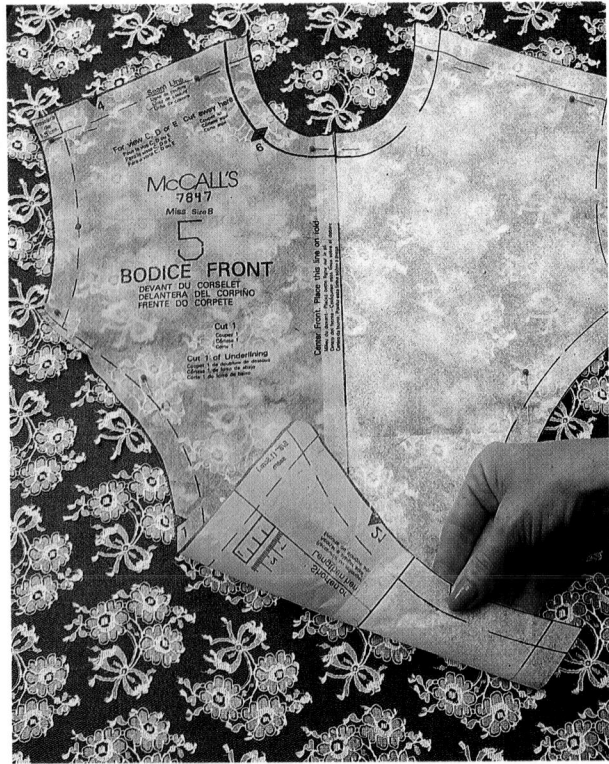

1) Work with full-sized pattern and single layer of fabric. First, pin front pattern in place, balancing prominent lace motifs within seamlines.

2) Cut around motifs beyond each lapped seamline with small, sharp scissors. Leave ¼" (6 mm) of background net around motifs. Manicure scissors with curved tips work well on fine laces.

3) Thread-trace seamlines with long and short basting stitches. Gently lift pattern off lace. Place front section on fabric, matching motifs, to determine the position for adjoining section.

4) Lap front seamline over seamline of adjoining pattern. Lace motifs will not always match exactly. Cut the adjoining section with ⅝" (1.5 cm) seam allowances. Thread-trace seamlines.

5) Lap garment edges on seamlines, front over back, matching thread-traced lines. Work from right side of garment. Baste layers together.

6) Straight-stitch or use narrow zigzag to stitch seam. Stitch next to outline of lace motifs to give them depth. (Contrasting thread is used to show detail.)

7) Clip the underlapping and overlapping seam allowances close to the lace motifs. Use small, sharp scissors.

Hem & Edge Finishes

To hem a lace garment, take advantage of the fabric's nonraveling nature and any built-in design motifs. If, during pattern layout, you are able to position pattern hems along lace borders for a self-hem, no further finish is needed. Some lace motifs can be clipped for a decorative hem edge even if they do not have a finished border. Hems using an edge of the motif as a finish are suitable only for patterns with straight hemlines.

Appliquéd hem provides a way to use a lace border on a neckline or flared pattern silhouette with a curved hemline. The border may be applied in a separate step. For an appliquéd hem, trim the lace border, motif, or lace edging, and lap it over the garment for the look of a self-hem.

Horsehair braid hem is used to stiffen the hem for a well-defined lower edge on bouffant gowns. It is a machine method that is quickly sewn and is suitable for softly draped silhouettes or lightweight laces.

How to Sew an Appliquéd Hem or Edge Finish

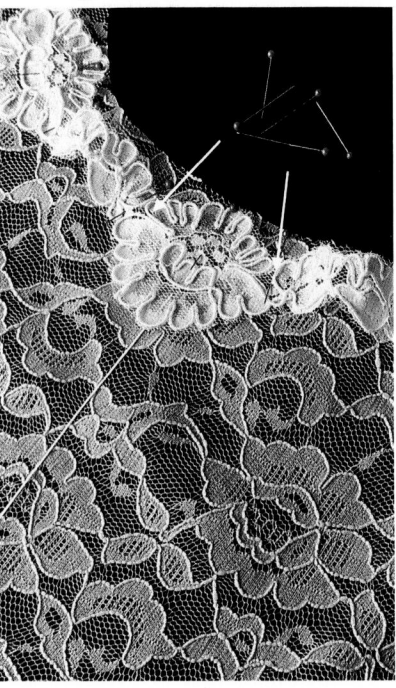

1) **Prepare** border by clipping near edges of lace motifs, leaving one or two rows of netting beyond edges. Use small, sharp scissors.

2) **Lap** border over garment, positioning inner points of scallops (arrows) on garment seamline or hemline. Place prominent border motif at center front. (Contrasting lace is used to show detail.)

3) **Clip** around border motifs, and lap cut edges slightly to shape border to neckline or hemline curve. Whipstitch lapped edges in place.

How to Sew a Horsehair Braid Hem

1) Mark hem on right side of garment, using water-soluble marking pen. Trim ½" (1.3 cm) below marking.

2) Stitch horsehair braid on right side of garment ¼" (6 mm) from edge, raw edges even. To prevent puckering, allow braid to relax as you sew.

3) Fold braid to inside of garment so ¼" (6 mm) hem wraps over edge. Press hem fold lightly. Stitch in the ditch between hem and horsehair, or hand-tack to seams.

4) Piece border if necessary by clipping around motifs and lapping edges as in step 3, left. Handle border seams the same way.

5) Stitch inner edge of border to garment with hand whipstitches if intricately shaped or with machine zigzag stitches if simply shaped. (Contrasting thread is used to show detail.)

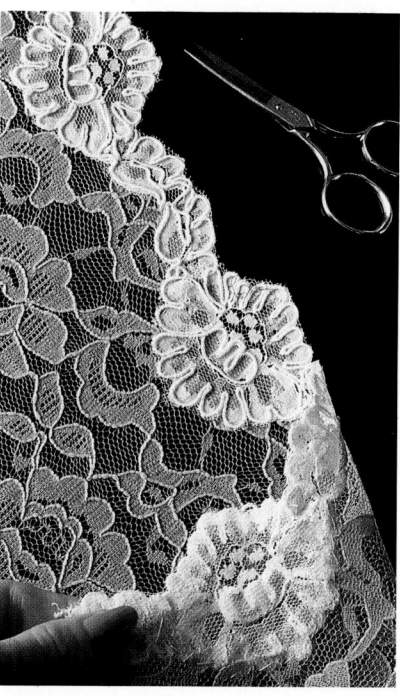

6) Trim underlapping garment hem or seam allowance ⅛" to ¼" (3 to 6 mm) from stitching. Work from inside of garment, using small, sharp scissors.

Lace Appliqués

Lace appliqués, either purchased as single medallions or cut from lace fabric, make elegant trims on special-occasion garments. These trims are often used as accents on bridal and evening gown bodices when the skirt is cut from lace fabric. They can also be used as feminine details on silky lingerie and blouses.

Three different methods can be used to apply individual lace motifs to a garment. To stitch appliqués in place, use either the hand or machine method. Another quick technique is securing appliqués with fusible web. This method is suitable for laces and background fabrics that are not sensitive to heat and steam.

Attaching Lace Appliqués

Use lace fabric. Clip around lace motif. Leave one or two rows of net around edges to give motif definition and to keep re-embroidered lace cordings from raveling. Or purchase lace appliqué.

Hand-stitch. Use short running stitches ¼" (6 mm) from appliqué edges. Keep stitches loose so background fabric stays smooth and appliqué is not flattened. (Contrasting thread is used to show detail.)

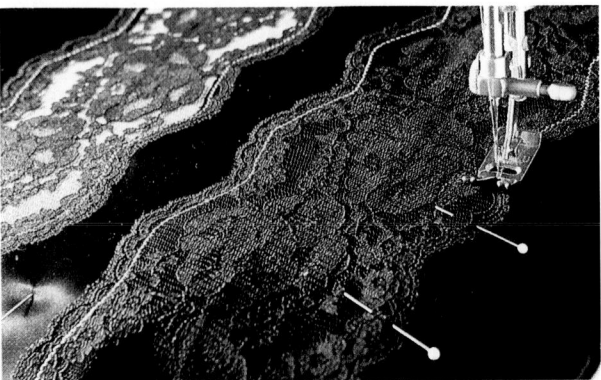

Machine-stitch. Use a narrow zigzag or short straight stitch ¼" (6 mm) inside edges. Under the motif, trim fabric close to zigzag stitching for sheer effect. (Contrasting thread is used to show detail.)

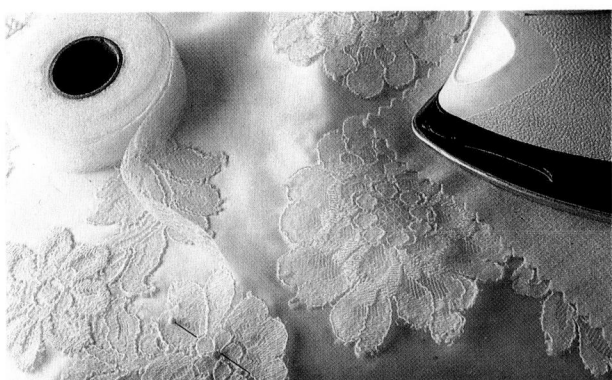

Fuse. Position garment, right side up, on covered pressing surface. Place appliqué on garment. Slip circles of fusible web under appliqué. Cover with paper towels or absorbent press cloth. Fuse, following manufacturer's directions.

Lustrous Fabrics

The lustrous surface of special occasion fabrics can come from the weave of the fabric, as is true for satin, or from fibers with sheen, such as silk and acetate. Special finishes also create surface luster, or metallic yarns or sequins can be added to give an ordinary fabric glamorous sparkle.

1) Satin is a weave that produces a shiny surface texture from floating yarns. The combination of fibers such as silk, rayon, or polyester with the distinctive weave makes the fabric likely to water-spot; protect the fabric with a press cloth, and use a dry iron when pressing. Use superfine pins to avoid snagging surface yarns.

2) Crepe-backed satin is also called satin-backed crepe because the fabric is reversible; one face has the matte, pebbly texture of crepe, and the other face has the smooth, shiny texture of satin. One side may be used as a binding or trim for the other.

3) Satin peau is a satin with a firm twill weave on the right side. Some peaus are double faced, with fine crosswise ribs on both sides. Because pins and ripped-out stitches can leave marks, pin only in seam allowance; test-fit to avoid ripping stitches.

4) Taffeta has a crisp hand and drapes stiffly. Test sewing techniques on scraps, because pins and ripped-out stitches can leave marks. When the fiber content includes acetate, steam can leave spots.

5) Moiré taffeta is passed between heated rollers to give it a watermarked surface texture.

6) Brocade comes in all weights, from light to heavy, and has raised tapestry-style motifs. The motifs should be balanced on major garment sections and matched at prominent seams. Most brocades are woven, but some are knit. Careful pressing on a padded surface preserves the surface texture. When brocades have shiny metallic threads, set the iron at a low temperature for pressing. To make metallic brocades more comfortable, underline with batiste.

7) Metallic fabrics have metallic yarns woven or knit into them. Most metallics are sensitive to heat and discolor when steam is used. Finger press seams with a thimble or blunt end of a point turner; or use a cool, dry iron.

8) Lamé is a smooth, shiny metallic fabric, either knit or woven. Knit metallics drape and ease better than the wovens. Besides traditional gold, silver, and copper tones, lamé is available in iridescent colors.

9) Sequined fabrics have a knit or sheer woven base. A simple pattern style is especially important for these fabrics. Or use sequined fabric for only a part of the garment, such as the bodice.

Techniques for Lustrous Fabrics

Many fabrics fit into the lustrous category, and some have unique sewing requirements. However, all of these fabrics are alike in two ways: A "with nap" pattern layout is used for uniform color shading in the finished garment, and the less handling, the better. Keep handling to a minimum by choosing patterns in simple styles with few seams and darts. Avoid buttoned closings and details such as shaped collars and welt pockets. Use a simple pinked finish on plain seams, or treat raw edges with liquid fray preventer instead of using elaborate dressmaker techniques. Take special care when pressing, using a light touch and covering the pressing surface with a scrap of self-fabric so nap faces nap. To prevent ridges when pressing seams, press over a seam roll or place strips of heavy brown paper between seam allowance and garment.

Guide to Sewing Lustrous Fabrics

Equipment & Techniques	Mediumweight Crepe-backed satin, lamé, satin, satin peau, silk, taffeta, moiré	Heavily Textured Brocade, sequined fabrics
Machine Needles	Size 11 (75)	Size 14 (90) or 16 (100)
Stitch Length	8 to 12 per inch (2.5 cm)	8 to 12 per inch (2.5 cm)
Millimeter Stitch Setting	3.5 to 2.5	3.5 to 2.5
Thread	All-purpose cotton or cotton/polyester, silk for silk fabrics	All-purpose cotton or cotton/polyester
Hand Needles	Betweens, size 7 or 8	Betweens, size 7 or 8
Interfacings	Sew-in nonwoven or woven	Sew-in nonwoven or woven
Special Seams	Plain seam: pinked, overedge, three-step zigzag, or liquid fray preventer finish	Plain seam or lined to edge
Special Hems	Catchstitched, topstitched, horsehair braid, faced	Faced

Tips for Handling Lustrous Fabrics

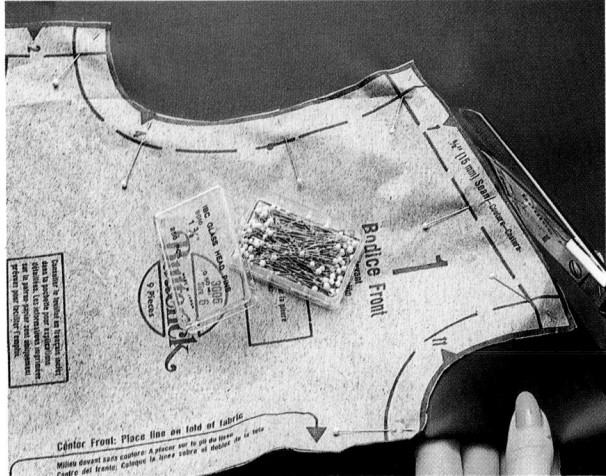

Layout. Pin only in seam allowances to prevent pin marks. Use extra-fine silk pins for finely woven fabrics such as satin and taffeta. Shears must be sharp or strokes will chew raw edges of fabric. Cut directionally for smoothest edges. Always use "with nap" layout for fabrics with luster.

Seams. Use plain seams with a simple edge finish. Raw edges can be pinked, overlocked, or finished with three-step zigzag. If fabric frays easily, apply thin coat of liquid fray preventer to raw edges. Slip envelopes between seam allowances and garment to protect garment from stray drops.

Hems

Four hemming techniques are recommended for lustrous fabrics. The most versatile hand-sewn hem is catchstitched. The crisscrossing stitches are flexible and worked blind, between hem edge and garment. This prevents the hem edge from making a ridge on the right side.

To put in hems quickly by machine, make either the topstitched hem or the horsehair braid hem. Because the topstitching method shows on the right side, it is most suitable for underskirts, which will be covered by lace or another sheer outer fabric, or if you can, cover the topstitching with trim. Horsehair braid makes a stiffened hem, which is used on bouffant skirts.

A faced hem is practical when the fabric is too crisp or bulky to turn under, such as satin peau or sequined fabrics. Use purchased hem facing or cut 2" (5 cm) wide bias strips from lightweight fabric to substitute for the self-fabric hem allowance.

Adjust the depth of the hem allowance according to the amount of flare in the pattern silhouette. A 2" (5 cm) hem is deep enough to help straight styles drape properly. On flared styles, the hem should be no more than 1" (2.5 cm) deep to eliminate excess fabric which must be eased at curves. On full or circular styles, use a narrow ¼" to ½" (6 mm to 1.3 cm) machine-stitched hem to reduce excess fabric even further.

Hems for Lustrous Fabrics

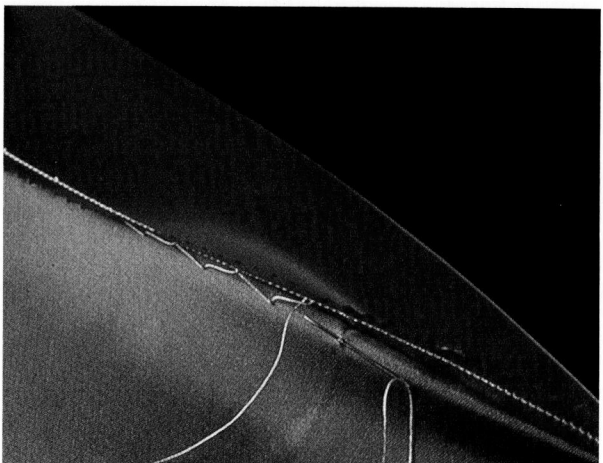

Catchstitched. Stitch and pink raw hem edge. Fold raw edge down, and catchstitch between garment and raw edge. Keep stitches loose for flexible, invisible hem. Press lightly.

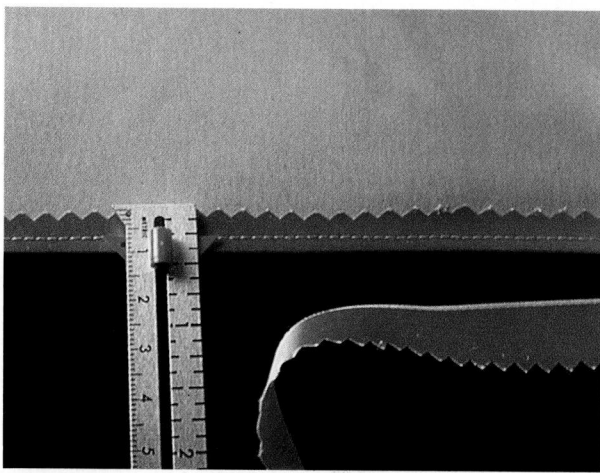

Topstitched. Press hem; then pink raw edge to trim hem depth according to pattern silhouette. Topstitch so stitches fall ¼" (6 mm) from pinked edge.

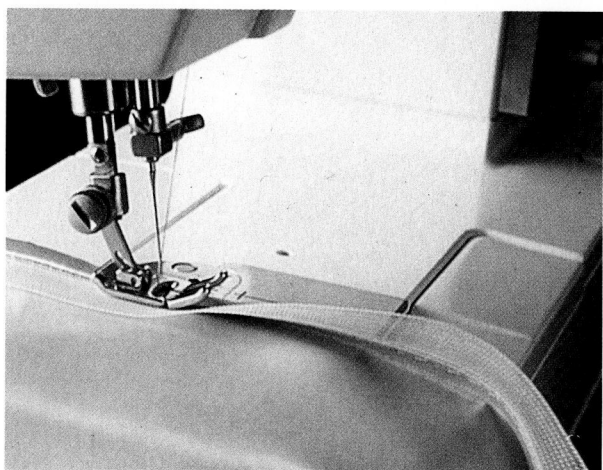

Horsehair braid. Trim hem ½" (1.3 cm) below hemline. Stitch horsehair braid ¼" (6 mm) from edge on right side. Press braid to wrong side. Stitch in the ditch or hand-tack at seamlines (page 51).

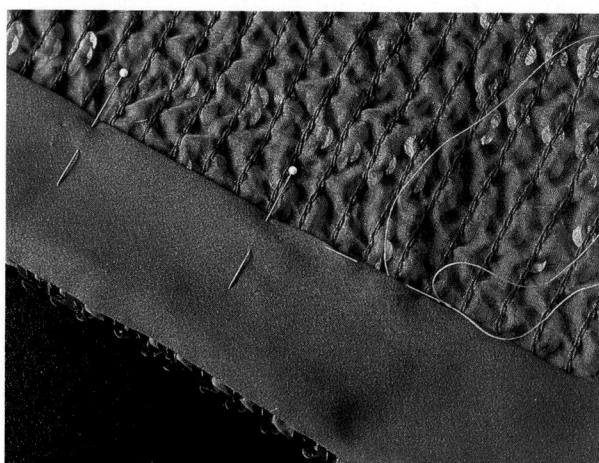

Faced. Stitch bias hem facing to garment on hemline with ¼" (6 mm) seam. Loosely slipstitch upper edge of facing to garment by hand.

Closures

Give special attention to center back zipper insertions in bridal and evening garments so these closures enhance rather than detract from the appearance. Because machine stitching can cause the fabric to pucker on each side of the zipper, use the hand prickstitch. To help zippered closures lie flat and smooth on fitted gowns, add a waistline stay. Fit the stay slightly tighter than the bodice to take strain off the zipper.

Small buttons and loops are a traditional closure on a bridal gown, and they can be made three ways. The fastest method is the mock closure; the buttons are sewn to the lapping side of a zipper to imitate the look of buttons and loops. For a working button/loop closing, omit the zipper and use either purchased looped trim or make the loops with self-fabric or thin soutache braid.

Tips for Sewing Zippers on Gowns

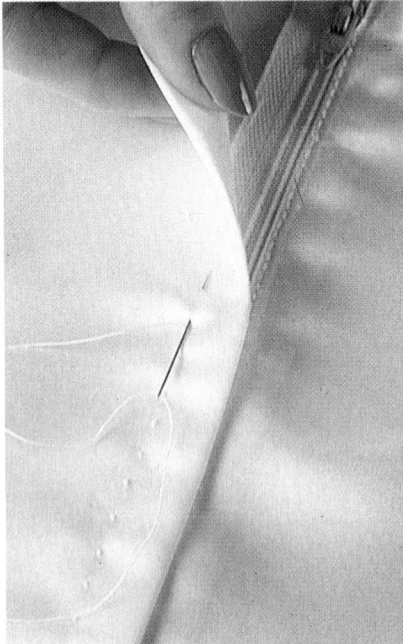

Prickstitch. Insert zipper by hand, using tiny backstitches spaced ⅛" to ³⁄₁₆" (3 to 5 mm) apart. Nylon or silk thread slips between yarns of tightly woven fabrics and makes invisible stitches.

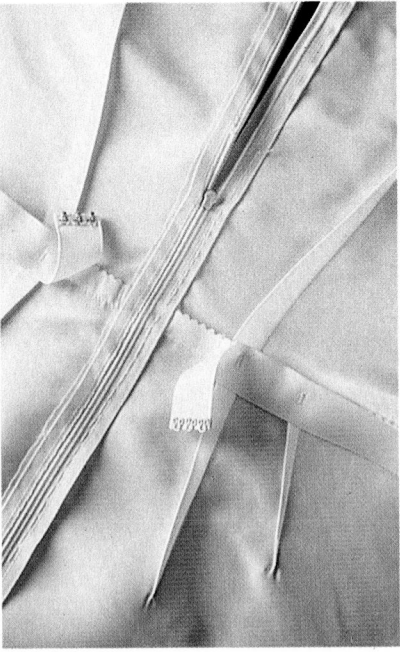

Waistline stay. Tack grosgrain ribbon to side seams and darts or to waistline seam allowance. Fasten stay with hooks and eyes under zipper. Fit stay slightly tighter than bodice to take strain off zipper.

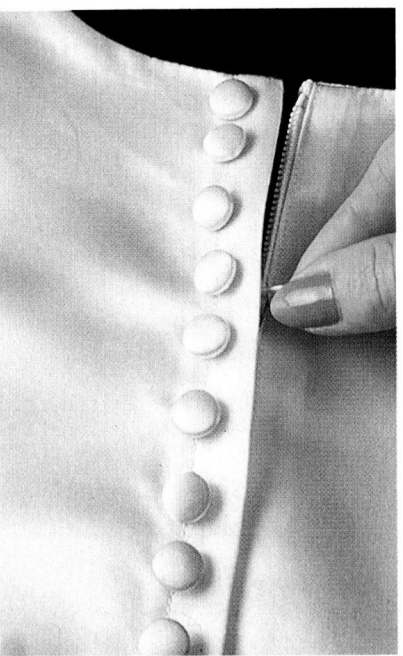

Mock button/loop closure. Cover lapped side of zipper closure with row of buttons, spaced ⅛" to ¼" (3 to 6 mm) apart. When zipped, closure looks like traditional button/loop closing.

How to Sew Button Loops

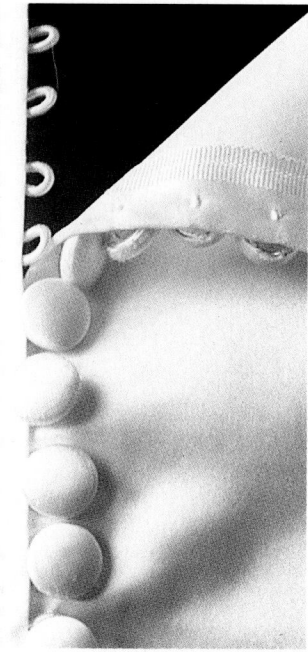

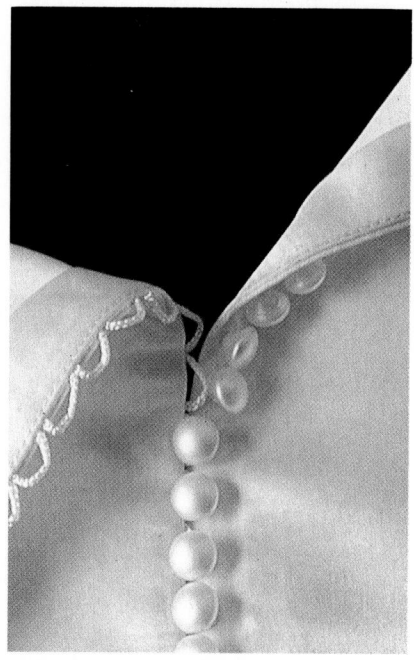

1) Fold under seam allowance on right side (overlap) of seam. Press. Baste looped trim ⅛" (3 mm) from fold, on inside of seam, so loops extend beyond edge. Use two strips for closer spaced buttons.

2) Stitch next to edge of trim. Fold under seam allowance on left side of seam, and sew buttons through both layers of fabric.

Alternative method. Pin loop tape on seam allowance on right side of garment, with loops toward garment. Pin narrow facing over loops. Stitch seam; fold to wrong side. Also stitch facing on the button side of closure.

How to Make Soutache Braid Loops

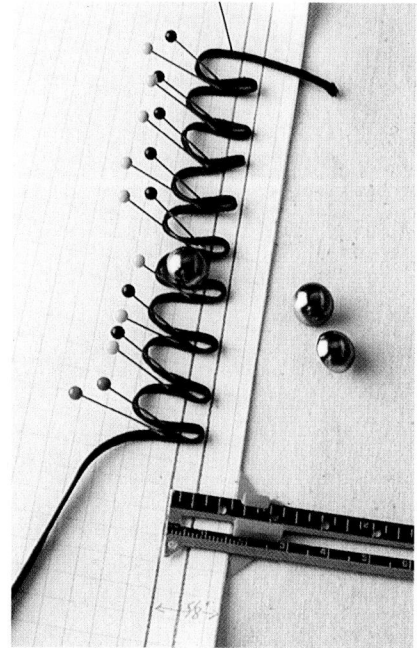

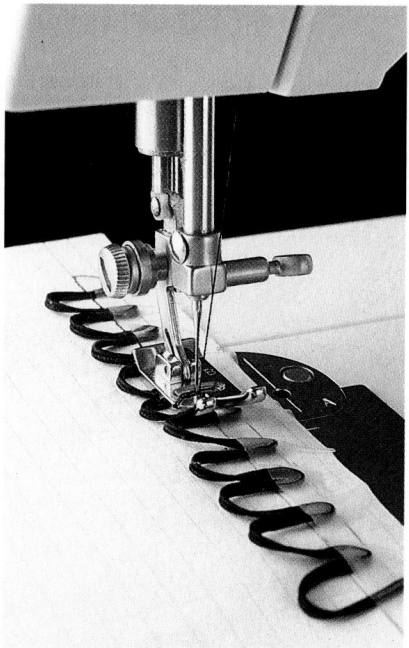

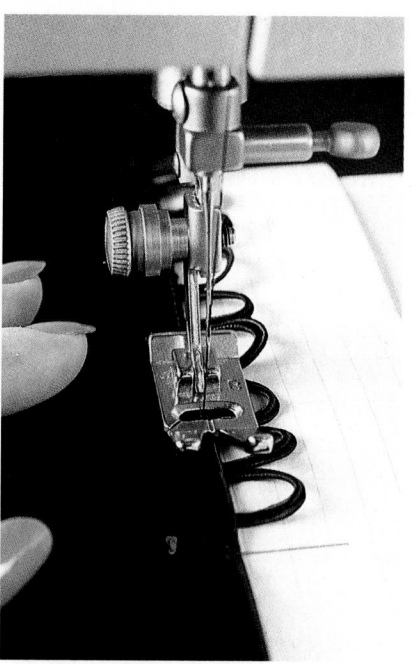

1) Form continuous series of loops on ¼" (6 mm) graph paper. Make each loop ½" (1.3 cm) long and deep enough to fit the button. Mark ⅝" (1.5 cm) seam allowance on paper.

2) Tape loops into position with transparent tape. Machine-baste base of loops, stitching through braid and graph paper. Leave paper in place; remove tape.

3) Stitch loops to right side of garment, with edge of paper matching raw edge of seam. Fold seam allowance back; edgestitch. Tear off graph paper. Sew buttons in place, as shown above.

Techniques for Sequined & Metallic Fabrics

Sequined fabrics are most easily used for garments that are simple in style with an easy, pullover fit. Avoid zippers, buttonholes, darts, pleats, or gathers. The background fabric may be sheer and light-weight, such as chiffon, or elasticized for a snug, stretchy fit. Either weight can also be used for accent, such as sleeves, bodice, collar, or cuffs.

Linings, Facings & Interfacings

Because sequins and metallics are irritating when worn next to the skin, line the garment or section fully so seam allowances are covered. Cut facings from lining fabric, or line to the edge, to reduce bulk and protect your skin. Face hems with lining fabric or purchased bias hem facing.

When interfacing is needed to support necklines or other garment edges, use a sew-in interfacing compatible with the weight of the base fabric. Fusible interfacings cannot be used on heat-sensitive metallic or sequined fabrics.

Care

Like many luxury textiles, sequined and metallic fabrics require special care. Treat the finished garment tenderly, and do not let chemicals from perfumes, grooming aids, or alcoholic beverages come in contact with the sequins. Use a professional drycleaner when the garment becomes soiled; ask that the garment be dried without heat and not pressed or steamed. Do not store the garment in a plastic bag.

How to Press

Use caution when pressing metallics and sequins because they are heat sensitive. Instead of traditional pressing methods, press with the blunt end of a point turner or finger press with a thimble. Run your finger or the point of the turner along the seamline. For final pressing, use a low temperature setting on the iron, and run the tip along the seamline only. Do not use steam; it removes the sheen from sequins and metallic threads.

Layout, Cutting & Marking

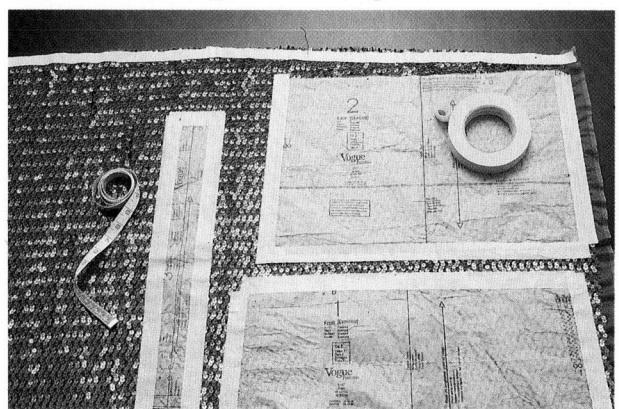

1) Place all pattern pieces in same direction for a "with nap" layout. Sequins should run down toward bottom edge of garment or garment section. Use masking tape to hold pattern on fabric. Work with single layer of fabric, right side up.

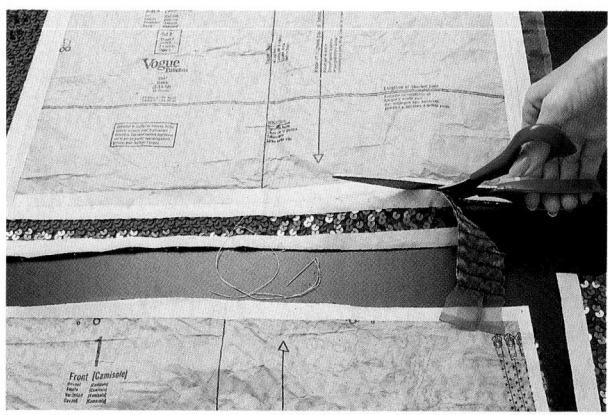

2) Cut through masking tape and fabric around each pattern piece; tape secures sequins at raw edges and prevents flying fragments as you cut. Anchor the pattern pieces with pins. Transfer pattern markings to back of fabric with thread tracing or tailor's tacks.

How to Sew a Seam on Sequined Fabrics

1) Staystitch cutout garment sections on seamlines immediately after cutting. This prevents loss of sequins. Stitch directionally, right side up so feed dog does not catch on sequins. Use sharp size 14 (90) or 16 (100) needle on sewing machine.

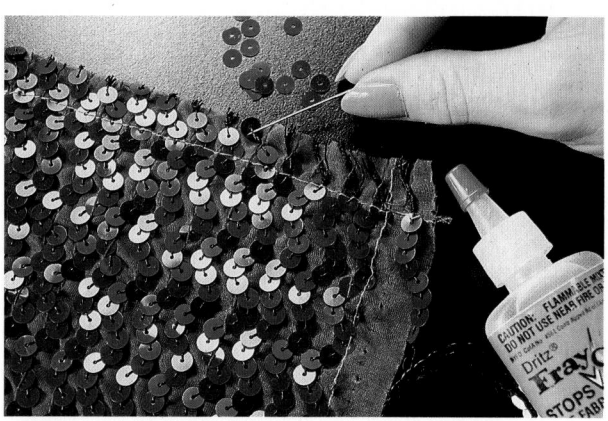

2) Remove loose sequins from seam allowances by slipping them off threads; save these sequins for repairs. To secure threads, seal to base fabric with liquid fray preventer.

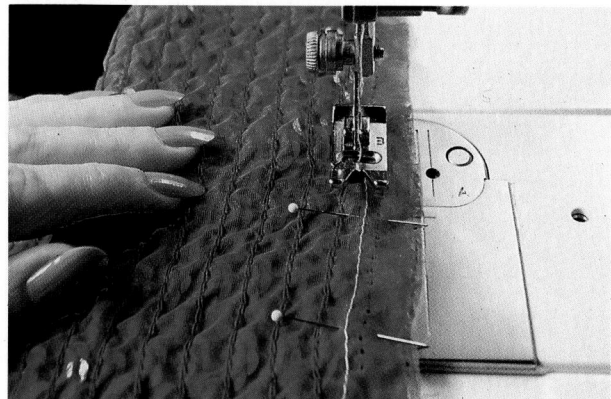

3) Stitch seam, using long stitches, 8 to 10 per inch (2.5 cm). Replace needle with new one frequently because sequins dull needle points rapidly.

4) Check right side of seam. Use reserved sequins to replace any sequins broken during stitching. Use fine hand-sewing needle and fine thread to sew sequins individually in place.

Classic Fabrics

Classic Fabric Textures & Designs

Whether or not you have had much sewing experience, this group of fabrics probably looks familiar because it includes fabrics that are always in fashion. Some require out-of-the-ordinary sewing techniques, and some need special handling because they have unique surface textures. Others rate extra attention because they have woven, knitted, or printed designs that affect pattern layout.

1) Loose weaves have coarse or uneven textures and tend to fray. The primary sewing challenge with loosely woven fabrics is to control raveling.

2) Plaids require careful pattern layout. Study the fabric before pattern layout to decide which bars are dominant, where to position them on the pattern pieces, and whether the design has a one-way direction. Arrange the pattern pieces so the fabric design matches at the most noticeable seams. Careful pinning or basting ensures against mismatches.

3) Stripes require handling similar to that of plaids. Careful layout and basting is necessary to match stripes attractively.

4) Large prints are among the most dramatic types of fabric designs. Print repeats can be as large as 24" (61 cm). With prints this size, position the print motifs for pleasing balance.

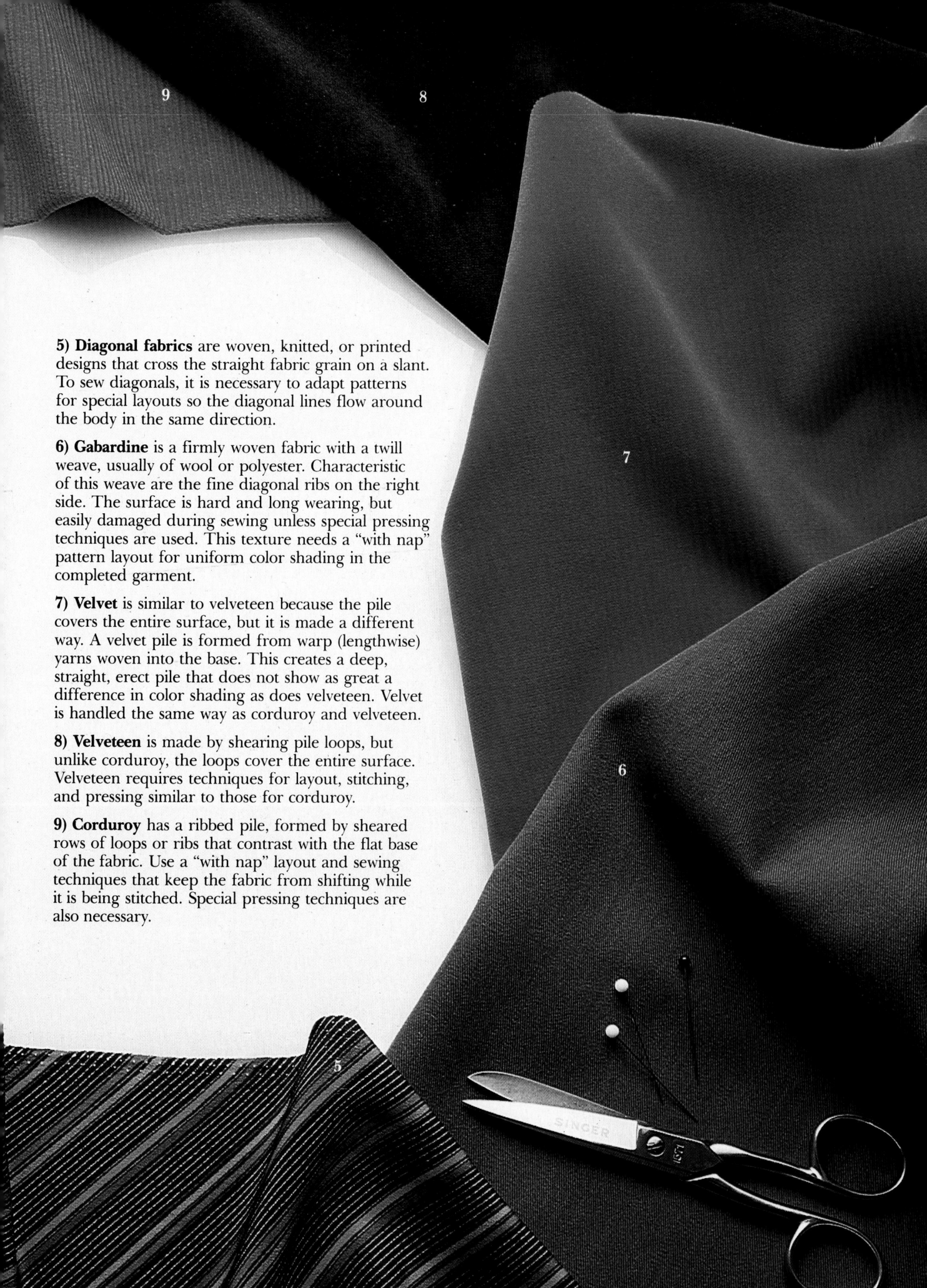

5) Diagonal fabrics are woven, knitted, or printed designs that cross the straight fabric grain on a slant. To sew diagonals, it is necessary to adapt patterns for special layouts so the diagonal lines flow around the body in the same direction.

6) Gabardine is a firmly woven fabric with a twill weave, usually of wool or polyester. Characteristic of this weave are the fine diagonal ribs on the right side. The surface is hard and long wearing, but easily damaged during sewing unless special pressing techniques are used. This texture needs a "with nap" pattern layout for uniform color shading in the completed garment.

7) Velvet is similar to velveteen because the pile covers the entire surface, but it is made a different way. A velvet pile is formed from warp (lengthwise) yarns woven into the base. This creates a deep, straight, erect pile that does not show as great a difference in color shading as does velveteen. Velvet is handled the same way as corduroy and velveteen.

8) Velveteen is made by shearing pile loops, but unlike corduroy, the loops cover the entire surface. Velveteen requires techniques for layout, stitching, and pressing similar to those for corduroy.

9) Corduroy has a ribbed pile, formed by sheared rows of loops or ribs that contrast with the flat base of the fabric. Use a "with nap" layout and sewing techniques that keep the fabric from shifting while it is being stitched. Special pressing techniques are also necessary.

Loose Weaves

Loosely woven fabrics are frequently made from unusual yarns, which are thick and lightly spun to preserve natural irregularities and create a hand-loomed look. Two sewing considerations are to control the raveling and to maintain the soft, loose hand of the fabric.

The loosely woven basketweave (1) has two or more yarns woven together in a basket effect. Heavy raw silk (2) is ravel-prone because of the thick and thin crosswise yarns. Gauze fabrics (3), lightweight and crinkly, should be handled with sewing techniques for sheer fabrics. The homespun look (4) is achieved with lightly spun yarns that ravel easily. A pulled thread look (5) creates a novelty windowpane effect.

Pattern Selection

Choose a pattern that has the potential for omitting linings, facings, and interfacings, as well as closures such as buttons and zippers. Many jacket, blouse, and skirt patterns, especially pullover or wrap styles, can be adapted this way. The less stable the fabric, the more loosely fitted the pattern selected should be, but in most cases simple styles are the best. The stability of loosely woven fabrics varies. Test the stability by draping the fabric over your hand and letting a length hang freely. See how much it stretches and whether it drapes softly. Gently tug on the true bias grain to get a feeling for the amount the fabric gives in this direction.

Fabric Preparation

Preshrink all loose weaves, using the care method planned for the finished garment. To prevent excessive raveling, zigzag crosswise cut ends or bind them with sheer bias tricot binding before washing. To wash, treat loose weaves like delicate fabrics. Air dry to prevent shrinkage from the heat of a dryer. Roll the fabric in towels to remove excess moisture. Spread on a flat surface, and straighten the grain.

Layout, Cutting & Marking

Because the individual yarns of the fabric stand out, it is important to arrange the fabric straight and on-grain for pattern layout. Any wavy grainlines will show clearly on the finished garment. When the fabric texture comes from nubby, irregular yarns, use a "with nap" layout so the texture in all the garment sections looks the same. Space pins closely to anchor the pattern pieces securely to the fabric.

If you are working with a fabric that frays readily, cut out the pattern with 1" (2.5 cm) seam allowances. Wider seam allowances are easier to handle for special seam and edge finishes, and they provide ample fabric for clean cuts on raw edges that must be trimmed. Transfer pattern markings with marking pen or thread basting.

Special Seam Techniques

Plain seam with raw edges enclosed in sheer tricot bias binding is quick, neat treatment. Use zigzag, 3-step zigzag, or long straight stitches, 10 to 12 per inch (2.5 cm).

Flat-fell seam, formed on right side of garment, makes reversible seam which is ideal for roll-up sleeves or other areas showing both faces of seams.

Overlocked seam, sewn on 4-thread overlock machine or 3-thread machine with a row of straight stitches, covers raw edges with thread.

Special Hem Techniques

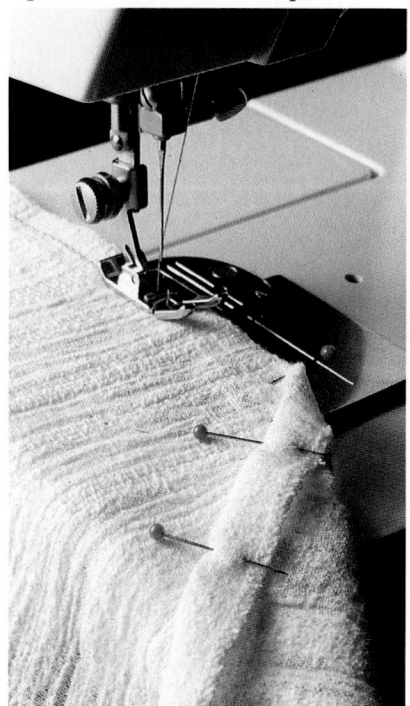

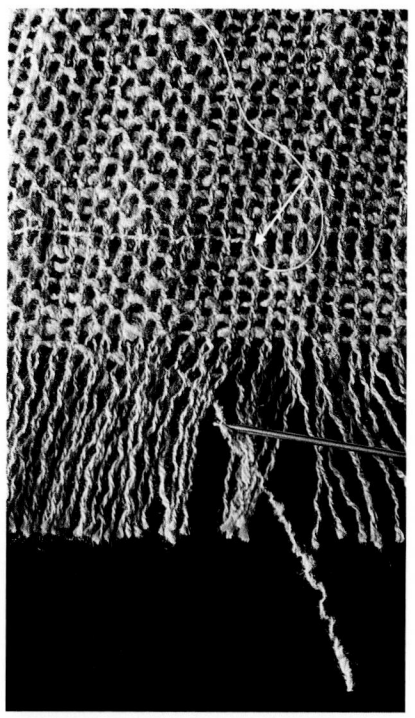

Topstitch to stabilize hem edges. This method is fast and attractive. Finish raw edge before hemming; use a zigzag stitch or a 2-thread or 3-thread overlock stitch.

Bind edge with sheer tricot bias binding. Hand hem with blind catchstitch or blind hem, worked loosely between garment and hem.

Fringe edge. Pull a thread at desired depth of fringe. Stitch on thread-pulled line (arrow); then one by one remove fabric yarns below stitching.

Corduroy & Velveteen

Corduroy, made from cotton or a blend of cotton/polyester fibers, comes in many forms. Corduroys are usually named according to the size and style of the ribs (wales).

1) Pinwale corduroy, also named baby wale or fine wale corduroy, is lightweight and has 16 ribs per inch (2.5 cm).

2) Midwale corduroy is heavier than pinwale and has fewer ribs.

3) Wide wale, also called jumbo wale, is a heavyweight corduroy with as few as three ribs per inch (2.5 cm).

4) Thick and thin corduroy is one of the many novelty variations with alternating sizes of ribs.

5) Ribless corduroy resembles the allover plush pile of velveteen.

Traditionally, corduroy is used for casual sports clothes and children's wear because it is durable and washable. Select patterns according to the form of corduroy you are using. The heavier the fabric and the bulkier the wales, the simpler the pattern style should be. Lightweight corduroys drape softly and can be used for more detailed styles, including those with gathered sections or ruffles. Midweight corduroys are often used for tailored jackets.

6) Velveteen, like corduroy, may be all-cotton or a cotton/polyester blend, but the texture is shorter and thicker than that of corduroy. Velveteen is a mediumweight fabric used whenever the look of velvet is desired. Velveteen is easier to sew and more durable than velvet.

Fabric Preparation

Preshrink corduroy and velveteen to prepare them for pattern layout. Tumble dry to fluff up the pile. This is especially important for all-cotton types, even though prewashing fades strong colors and can make the fabric look worn sooner. Polyester/cotton types shrink less, are less likely to fade, and shed wrinkles better than those made of all-cotton.

Stitching Tips

Pile fabrics such as corduroy and velveteen tend to shift as you stitch. An Even Feed™ foot or roller foot helps to prevent this. It is helpful to pin seams at close intervals and to practice taut sewing, holding the fabric under tension in front of and behind the presser foot. Stitch in the direction of the nap to keep the pile fabric texture smooth.

Some sewing machine adjustments may be needed for a smooth, balanced stitch. Use a long stitch, 10 to 12 per inch (2.5 cm), on most corduroys and velveteens. On thick, bulky corduroy, decrease pressure on the presser foot.

The raw edges of corduroy and velveteen ravel easily, so finish them with binding or overlocking. Grade enclosed seams to reduce bulk, but do not trim too closely. Enclosed raw edges can ravel unless topstitched or treated with liquid fray preventer.

Hem bulky or heavy corduroys and velveteen by hand. Or face the hem to reduce bulk. Use purchased hem facing, or cut 2" (5 cm) wide bias strips of polyester/cotton broadcloth.

Sewing Techniques for Corduroy and Velveteen

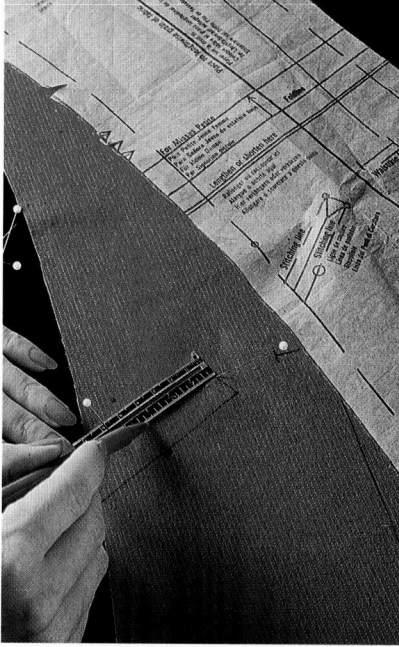

Decide which color shading you prefer before pattern layout. When nap feels smoother running up toward top of garment, color looks darker. When nap feels smoother running down toward garment hem, color looks lighter with slight sheen. Corduroy wears longer when nap runs down.

Mark cutout pattern sections with chalk and pins or marking pen; mark only on wrong side of fabric layers. Do not use tracing wheel and dressmaker's carbon paper without testing; tracing wheel can mar plush textures.

Press plush textures gently. Place self-fabric scrap, right side up, on pressing surface and place garment, right side down, on top. Press gently to avoid flattening pile. To prevent imprints on right side, use paper strips under seam allowances, or press seams open on a seam roll.

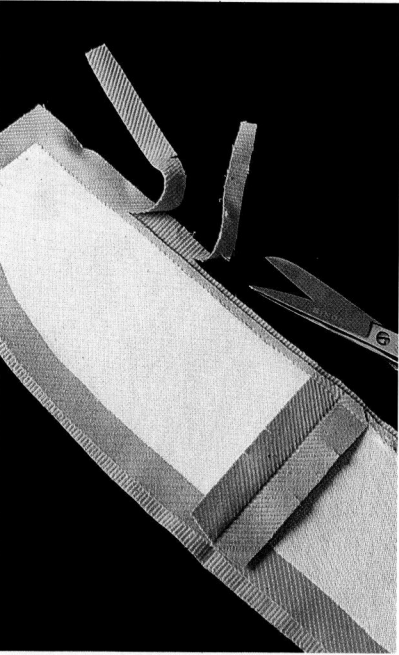

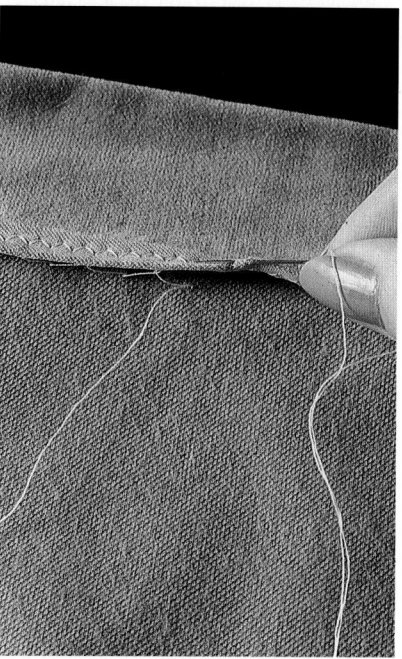

Finish all raw edges to prevent raveling. Use zigzag stitch **(a)**, bias binding **(b)**, or either 2-thread or 3-thread **(c)** overlock using extra-fine thread.

Grade enclosed seam allowances to reduce bulk. Optional topstitching may be placed far enough in from edge to enclose raw edges of graded seam. This prevents raveling and strengthens garment edges.

Hem with catchstitch. Bind, zigzag, or overlock raw hem edge to prevent raveling. Work blind catchstitch between hem and garment, using loose stitches to prevent hem imprint.

Velvet

The handling of velvet depends primarily on its fiber content. Cotton velvet, shown on the left, is made from all-cotton or a cotton/rayon blend. It has a fairly firm hand and tailors well for suits, jackets, and coats. Cotton velvet is resilient and can be stitched and pressed similar to velveteen. It can be machine washed, using mild detergent and a gentle cycle, and then tumble dried.

Lustrous velvets. Velvets made of rayon, acetate, or silk blends have a softer texture and hand than cotton velvet. Most of these velvets have a high luster (1). Handle the rich, lustrous pile carefully because it mars easily. Panne, the shiniest of the lustrous velvets, has a nap that is permanently pressed down during manufacturing (2). The flat nap adds to the sheen of the fabric. Drycleaning is necessary for all lustrous velvets.

Pattern Selection

The best patterns to use with velvet are softly draped silhouettes with a minimum of seams and darts and without buttonholes or topstitching. Velvet can be gathered or formed into unpressed pleats, and is often used for bridal and evening wear.

Layout, Cutting & Marking

Many apparel velvets are 39"/40" (100 cm) wide, a width rarely given in the fabric requirements on the back of a pattern envelope. To estimate how much velvet to buy, test the pattern layout at home or at the store, using a "with nap" layout.

In general, the less velvet is handled during the entire sewing project, the better. Make fitting changes on pattern pieces before layout; ripped-out seams leave marks.

Spread velvet, unfolded, right side up on the cutting surface. Lay out and cut the pattern pieces one layer of fabric at a time because velvet slips when folded: Cut facings from a lightweight lining fabric to keep bulk to a minimum. Cut the undercollar on a tailored garment from finely woven wool flannel to reduce bulk and to ensure a smoothly rolled collar.

Transfer only the essential pattern markings, using a marking pen or pins and chalk for symbols such as dots that show sleeve placement. As you sew, use the pattern tissue as an overlay to locate foldlines, pocket placement, and similar markings.

How to Lay Out Velvet

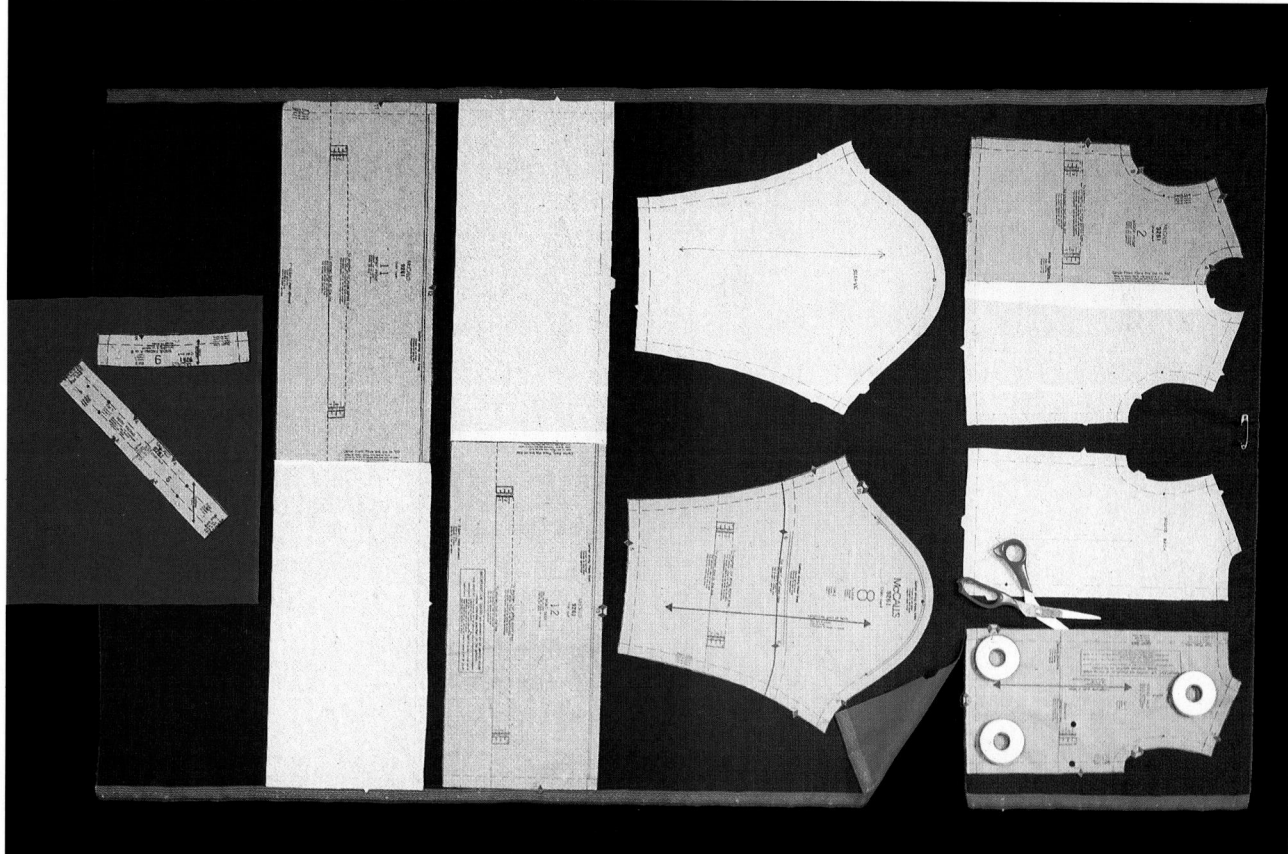

Mark direction of pile with safety pin at one crosswise edge, and place all pattern pieces in this direction. Lay out pattern on a single layer of fabric, positioning pattern pieces without pins until ready to cut. Working with one pattern piece at a time, pin in seam allowances only or use weights; cut in direction of the pile, toward safety pin marker. Cut around pattern notches; snipping seams to mark notches could cause a tear. Remove pins immediately after cutting out pattern section to prevent imprints on pile texture. Use lightweight woven fabrics for facings and undercollars.

Interfacings & Underlinings

Fusible interfacings can be used on cotton velvets if a test sample shows the pile is undamaged. To fuse, cover pressing surface with a velvet scrap, right side up, or a thick terry towel. Place test scrap plush side down for fusing. If pile looks crushed, use a sew-in interfacing. If a ridge shows at the edge of the interfacing, pink the edges of another sample of interfacing and test-fuse again. Pinking sometimes helps the interfacing edges to blend better with the pile. Use sew-in interfacings on lustrous velvets.

Underline cotton velvet with an easy-care fabric such as polyester/cotton batiste to prevent wrinkles. All velvets benefit from underlinings and gain support and strength from this extra fabric backing. Zigzag or overlock the raw edges of velvet and underlining together to finish the raw edges at the same time as you apply the two fabrics back to back. When overlocking an edge, mark notches with marking pen or chalk because they will be trimmed by the overlock stitch.

Pressing

All velvets require careful steam pressing to prevent flattening the pile, but extra caution is necessary with delicate lustrous velvets. Try finger pressing, wearing a thimble on your finger and lightly creasing the seam on the wrong side. Never rest the iron directly on velvet. Before handling, allow to dry completely.

Stitching Techniques

Two main problems in sewing velvet are puckered seams and uneven feeding of the fabric layers. Before you can achieve an acceptable seam, you may need to make some sewing machine adjustments.

Loosen the upper thread tension if puckers are a problem. Decrease the pressure on the presser foot if uneven feeding occurs, or try using an Even Feed™ or roller foot on your machine. Generous basting with pins, fine needles, or thread may be necessary as well. Stitching in the direction of the nap is always a good practice, and especially important with velvet, but cleaning the machine and inserting a new needle can make a difference, too.

Because velvet ravels, raw edges require finishing. In lined garments, pink the edges. In unlined garments, bind the edges with sheer tricot bias binding, or overlock them. Grade enclosed seam allowances to reduce bulk, but do not trim raw edges to less than ¼" (6 mm).

How to Stitch Velvet

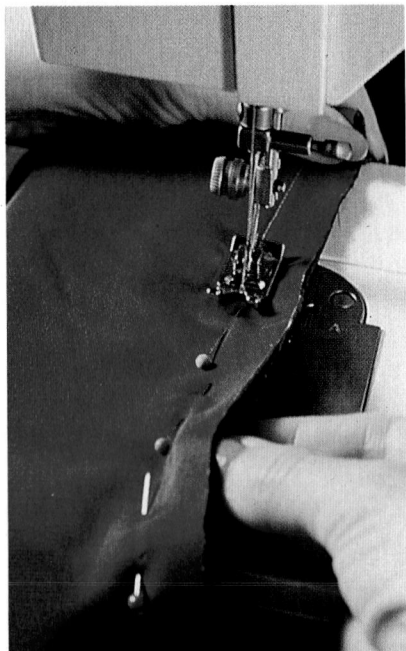

Pin-baste by placing pins parallel to seamline, with heads toward you. Do not stitch over pins, but remove them as you come to them. Use long stitches, 10 to 12 per inch (2.5 cm). As you sew, hold bottom fabric layer taut to encourage even feeding of seams.

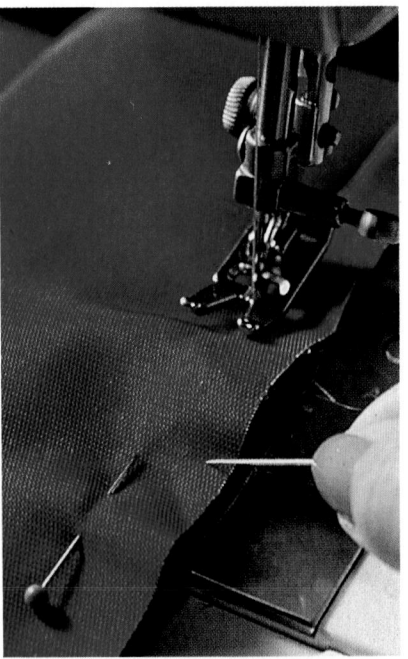

Stop stitching every 2" to 3" (5 to 7.5 cm). Raise presser foot with needle in fabric. Allow both fabric layers to relax. Lower presser foot and resume stitching. Use a pin to help ease the top layer along.

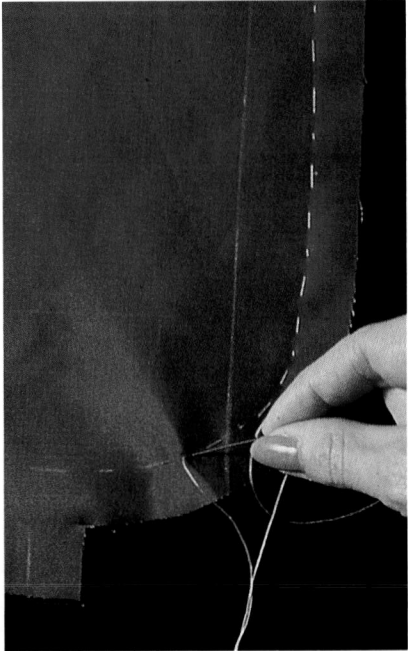

Hand-baste on curved seams that may be more difficult to handle. Use a fine thread, and backstitch every couple of inches (2.5 cm). Machine-stitch seam as directed at left, holding bottom layer taut.

How to Hem Velvet

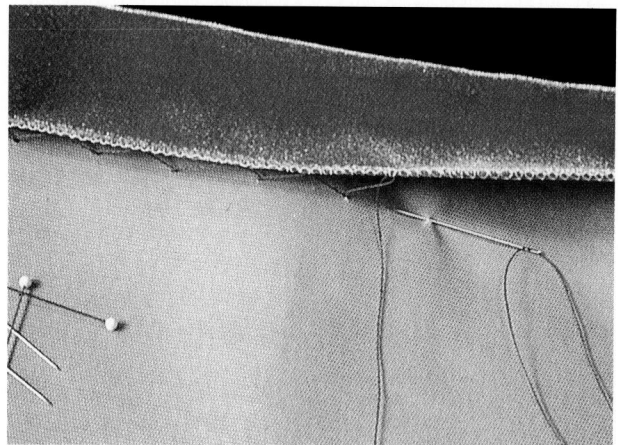

1) Finish the raw hem edge by overlocking or binding; then sew blind catchstitch hem between hem edge and garment, keeping the stitches loose.

2) Place hem on needle board or scrap of self-fabric. Steam hem from inside. To set hemline, pat along the foldline with a stiff-bristled brush.

Four Ways to Press Velvet

Cover pressing surface with velvet scrap, plush side up. Place garment with plush side down. Steam lightly, using hands to pat seam allowances. Never rest iron directly on velvet pile.

Use a needle board. Place velvet, pile side down, on needle board and press with steam iron or hand steamer from wrong side of garment.

Revive overpressed pile by steaming right side gently. Brush pile lightly with brush or scrap of fabric. Some piles may be permanently damaged.

Hang garment on a plastic or padded hanger in a steaming bathroom for about half an hour. Allow garment to dry thoroughly before handling.

Diagonal Designs

Almost every commercial pattern bears the warning "not suitable for obvious diagonals." Do not take the warning too literally. Sometimes patterns are labeled this way because there is not enough space in the pattern directions to include layouts for fabrics with diagonal designs. Some patterns can be adapted for use with these intriguing fabrics, even though you must work out the pattern layout.

Some fabrics have diagonal surface textures because of their twill weaves, but in the case of twills such as gabardine, denim, and flannel, the diagonal effect is hardly noticeable. When a diagonal fabric design is immediately obvious, you need to think about special patterns and layout techniques.

Pattern Selection

Consider shirt patterns with set-in sleeves and slim or gathered skirt patterns with seams on the straight fabric grain. Avoid seams that slant on the bias grain because diagonals will not meet at the same angle. Because of the way light reflects off the fabric

surface, diagonal weaves create odd optical illusions at seams if they are not on the straight fabric grain.

Naturally, the fewer seams there are, the easier the layout will be. Avoid patterns with fold-back lapels, raglan or dolman sleeves, shaped darts, and V-necklines; the diagonals either will not match or will look lopsided.

Pattern Layout

The key to pattern layout on diagonal fabrics is positioning the pattern pieces so the diagonal wraps around the garment in a continuous line. If a design runs from the left shoulder to the right hem on the garment front, it should also run from the left shoulder to the right hem in back. This is easier to visualize if you lay out and cut one garment section at a time on a single layer of fabric. Then you can position adjoining garment sections using the previously cut section, lining up the diagonal motif and matching it at as many seams as possible.

It is impossible to match the design at every seam, but mismatches are not a sign of amateur work. Designers who use diagonal fabrics give priority to achieving a flow of fabric design around the figure, not laboriously striving for perfectly matched seams.

How to Lay Out a Diagonal Design

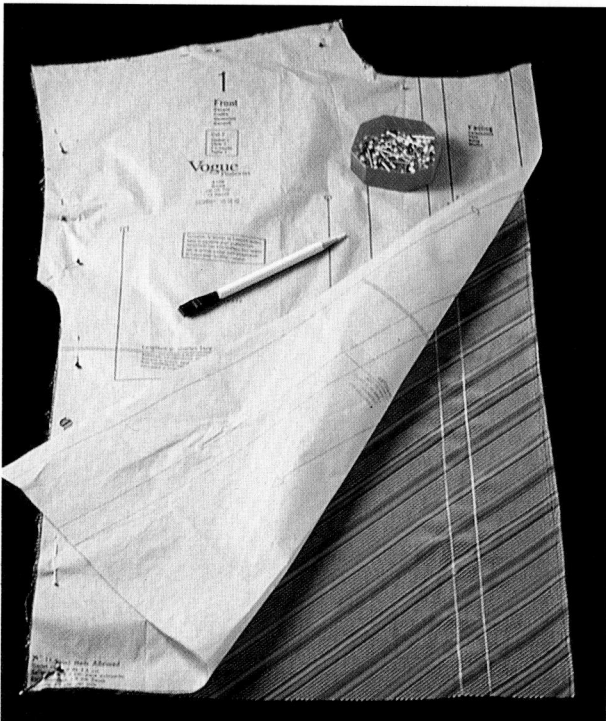

1) Pin a major pattern section, such as bodice front, to single layer of fabric; cut. Transfer pattern markings to cutout section. Unpin pattern and press foldlines.

2) Use cutout section to position other side of bodice front; flip pattern over to cut right and left sides. For garment with a center front opening, match diagonal line at the seamline or foldline, not the center front.

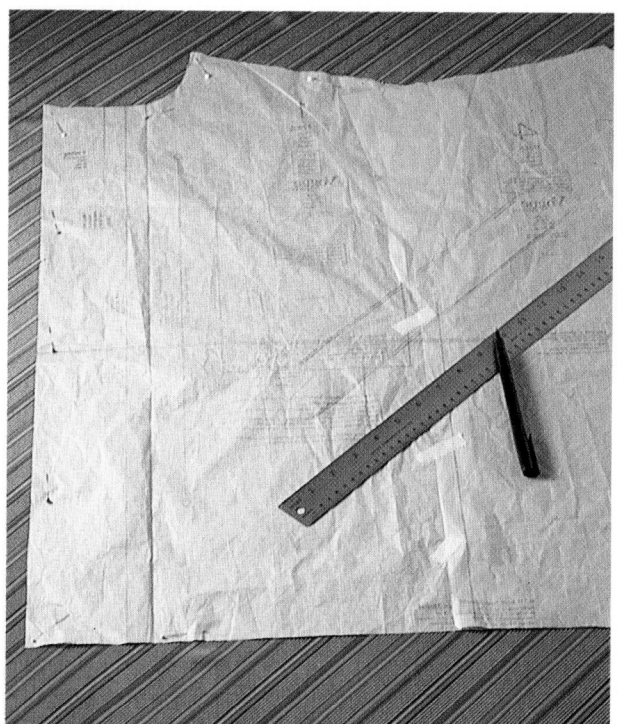

3) Cut out adjoining sections in similar way, working with one section at a time. Overlap side seams. Trace diagonal design onto pattern at side seams. Make sure design wraps continuously around garment.

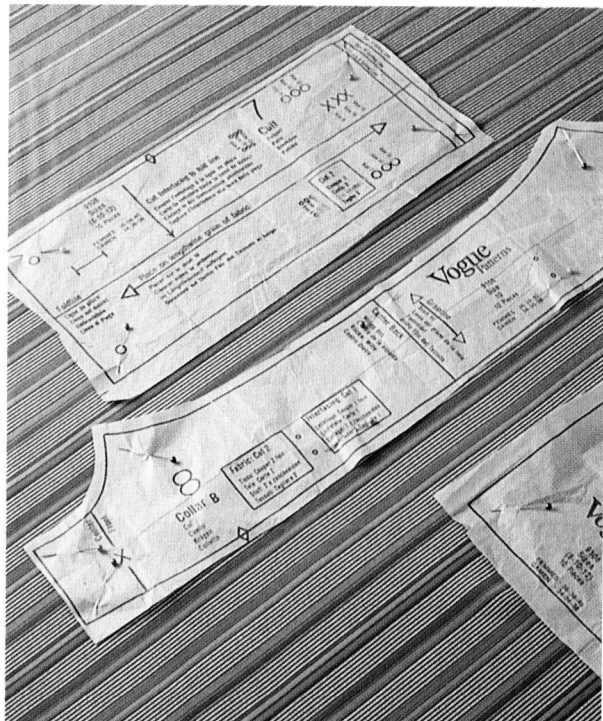

4) Cut cuffs, pockets, collars, or bindings on the bias for a vertical or horizontal contrast. If the diagonal design is not on a perfect bias 45° angle, use the design line as the cutting line.

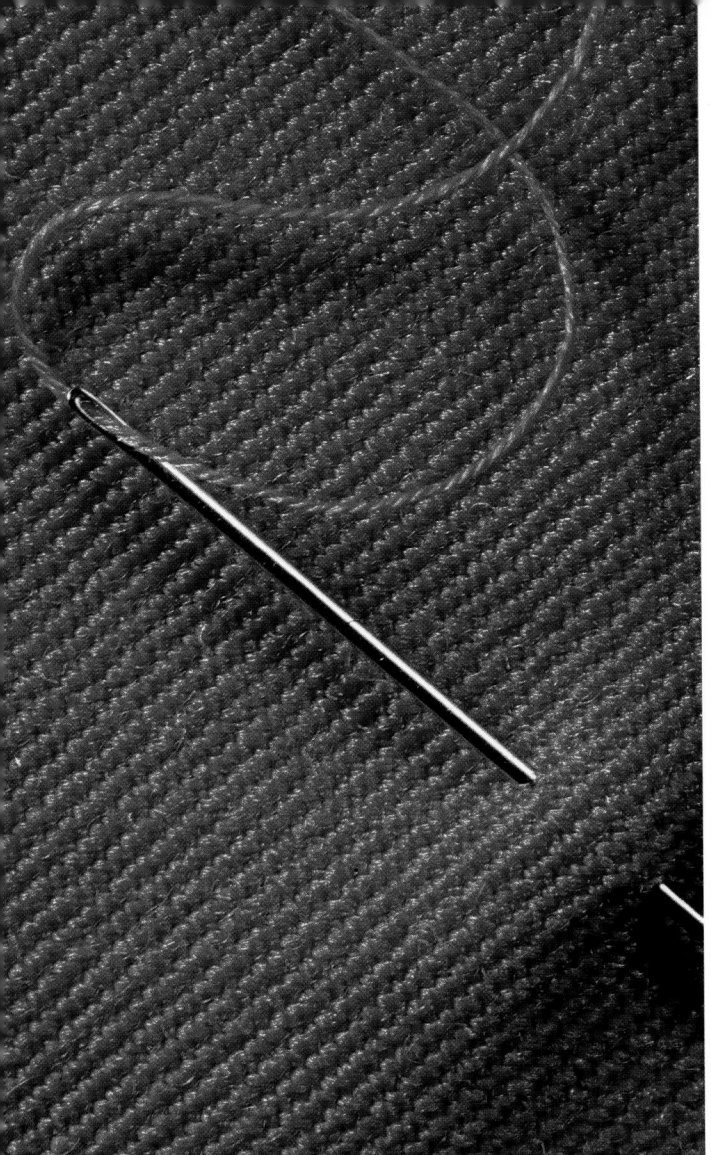

Gabardine

The firm, durable surface of gabardine is a strength of the fabric, but it is also the reason for special handling during sewing. The surface of gabardine is susceptible to damage during pressing. You can avoid problems if you press several times lightly rather than once with too much heat, moisture, and pressure. To prevent leaving imprints on the right side, place seams over a seam roll; press darts and shaped garment areas over a tailor's ham, using brown paper or envelopes under the dart. Always use a press cloth or iron soleplate cover when pressing on the right side of gabardine.

Fusible interfacings do not work on most gabardines, mainly because the firm weave will not admit the adhesives, but also because excessive steam and heat can make the gabardine look shiny. Use sew-in interfacings for gabardine garments.

Although the twill weave of a gabardine creates a diagonal line, this diagonal is barely noticeable except under a magnifying glass. It will not require a special layout to compensate for the diagonal; however, a "with nap" layout should be followed.

How to Press Seams on Gabardine

1) Press seam flat, as stitched. This embeds stitches into fabric. Do not slide iron; lift and lower it.

2) Arrange seam over seam roll or with strips of brown paper under seam allowances. Hold iron above fabric and saturate with steam. Do not touch iron to fabric surface.

3) Flatten seam with wooden clapper, forcing steam into the fabric. Do not pound. Allow fabric to cool and dry before handling.

Large Prints

Prints with repeats of up to 24" (61 cm) need special attention to pattern selection and layout. A large print may look overscaled in a small pattern size unless you are sewing a full-length skirt or dress that provides enough area for the print to be displayed effectively. Whatever size you sew, the fewer seams the pattern has, the fewer times the print will be interrupted and the more successful the finished garment will be.

Before starting the pattern layout, study the print. Most large prints are directional and require a "with nap" layout. Some prints also have a motif that must be placed so it is directed toward the neckline.

Decide where to position the prominent print motifs on major garment sections. Large motifs do not necessarily have to be centered on major pattern pieces, but they do have to be balanced. An uneven layout can be more pleasing than one where the motifs are centered on major garment sections. For example, when sewing a dress, you might place one large motif on the left shoulder, and another above the right hip. Drape the fabric over your figure, and study possible motif placements in front of a full-length mirror. Avoid putting a large print motif directly on the bustline or hipline, where it would look unflattering. Also, try to have a whole motif fall just above the hemline to create a balanced look.

Some large prints have motifs staggered in crosswise rows repeated regularly over the fabric length; for example, seven roses in a row, then five in a row. During layout, match like rows with like rows so the print flows continuously around the body.

Another concern in pattern layout is how the print flows from neckline to hem. If prominent print motifs are repeated every 12" (30.5 cm) and you have positioned a motif 2" (5 cm) above the waist seam of a dress, position another motif 10" (25.5 cm) below the waist seam for a balanced look.

Extra fabric is needed for creative pattern layouts on large prints. When motifs or repeats are spaced as far apart as 18" to 24" (46 to 61 cm), buy extra fabric equal to the spacing, ½ yd. to ¾ yd. (.50 to .70 m). When motifs or repeats are closer together, purchase one extra motif or repeat for each major pattern piece.

How to Lay Out Large Prints

Lay out pattern on single layer of fabric. Position major pattern pieces first, beginning with bodice front. Make sure motifs are balanced and in flattering positions.

Motifs of finished garment flow around garment and from neckline to hemline as well. Complete motifs are positioned at focal points, such as area above the hemline on garment front.

Plaids & Stripes

Plaid and striped fabrics require similar sewing techniques. Striped fabrics have bars of color running lengthwise or crosswise on the fabric. Plaids have color bars running lengthwise and crosswise.

Plaids and stripes need special pattern layouts to balance the arrangement of the color bars and to match the bars at important seams. Extra fabric is necessary for such a layout. The larger the plaid or stripe repeat, the more fabric is needed. The *repeat* of a plaid is the four-sided area that contains the complete design. The repeat of a stripe has two boundaries. For plaids, buy an additional repeat for each major pattern piece. For stripes, an extra ¼ yd. to ½ yd. (.25 to .50 m) is usually enough. Use the larger amount if the stripe is broad.

Add this allowance to the "with nap" fabric requirement if working with an uneven plaid or stripe. Patterns must be laid out on these one-way fabric designs in a single direction.

Determining Even & Uneven Plaids & Stripes

To decide whether a plaid is even or uneven, fold back one corner diagonally through the center of a repeat. If the color bars match diagonally, test the plaid one more way to make sure it is even. Fold a crease lengthwise and crosswise through the center of one repeat. If all quarters are identical, the plaid is even. If not, the plaid is uneven. A plaid can be uneven crosswise, lengthwise, or both. Some uneven plaids will pass the diagonal test but fail the lengthwise/crosswise test.

To decide whether a stripe is even or uneven, fold through the center of one repeat. If both halves are the same, the stripe is even. If not, it is uneven. Uneven stripes can be difficult to spot; sometimes the size and arrangement of the stripes are the same on both halves of one repeat, but the colors are different.

Selecting Patterns

The fewer seams and details a pattern has, the easier it is to use with plaids or stripes. Once you have had some experience handling these fabrics,

Identifying even and uneven plaids. An even plaid has lengthwise and crosswise color bars that match when the repeat is folded diagonally through the center (**1**). An uneven plaid may have differing color bars in one or more directions (**2**). Or an uneven plaid may have matching color bars but not form a mirror image when folded diagonally because the repeat is not square (**3**). This type of uneven plaid is the most difficult to identify.

however, you can place few limits on your pattern selection. In fact, when working with striped fabric, you may prefer a pattern with many details. By cutting sections such as yokes, cuffs, patch pockets, and applied bands crosswise, lengthwise, or on the true bias grain, you can run the stripes in contrasting directions to the stripes on the main body of the garment. This is an easy way to create a garment with a couture look.

Some pattern features to avoid when working with stripes and plaids are seams with eased areas, such as princess seams and diagonal or horizontal bustline darts, which interrupt the straight lines of the color bars. Occasionally, a pattern has a warning, "not suitable for plaids and stripes" because the shape of the seams prevents an acceptable match.

Matching Plaids & Stripes

For pattern layout, position the pattern pieces so stripes or plaids match at major seams. Lay out the large pattern pieces first, beginning with the front. Use a "with nap" layout if working with an uneven plaid or stripe. Place the center front on the most noticeable stripe so the garment will look balanced. With even plaids, you have the option of placing the center front of pattern pieces through the center of a repeat.

Lay out adjoining pattern pieces so the stripe or plaid matches at the most noticeable seams. Use the notches as your guide, remembering to match the fabric design at the seamline, not the cutting line. It may not be realistic to match every seam in a garment. Attempt to match the design at the front, back, and side seams, and at the front notches where set-in sleeves join the armholes. When seams have eased areas or darts, the entire seam will not match. Begin to match the stripe or plaid below the eased area or dart.

Lay out small straight-edged pattern pieces such as yokes, cuffs, and bands so one dominant color bar runs along the finished edge or through the center. Position details, such as patch pockets and collars, so the striped or plaid fabric design flows uninterrupted from garment to detail. Or, to eliminate having to match these details, place them on the true bias.

Identifying even and uneven stripes. An even stripe has matching color bars on each side when the dominant stripe is folded through the center (**1**). An uneven stripe has different color bars in each half of the repeat. Striped fabrics can be uneven because of the one-way sequence of stripe colors (**2**). Stripes can also be uneven because of the one-way sequence of stripe colors *and* widths (**3**).

How to Lay Out Even Plaids

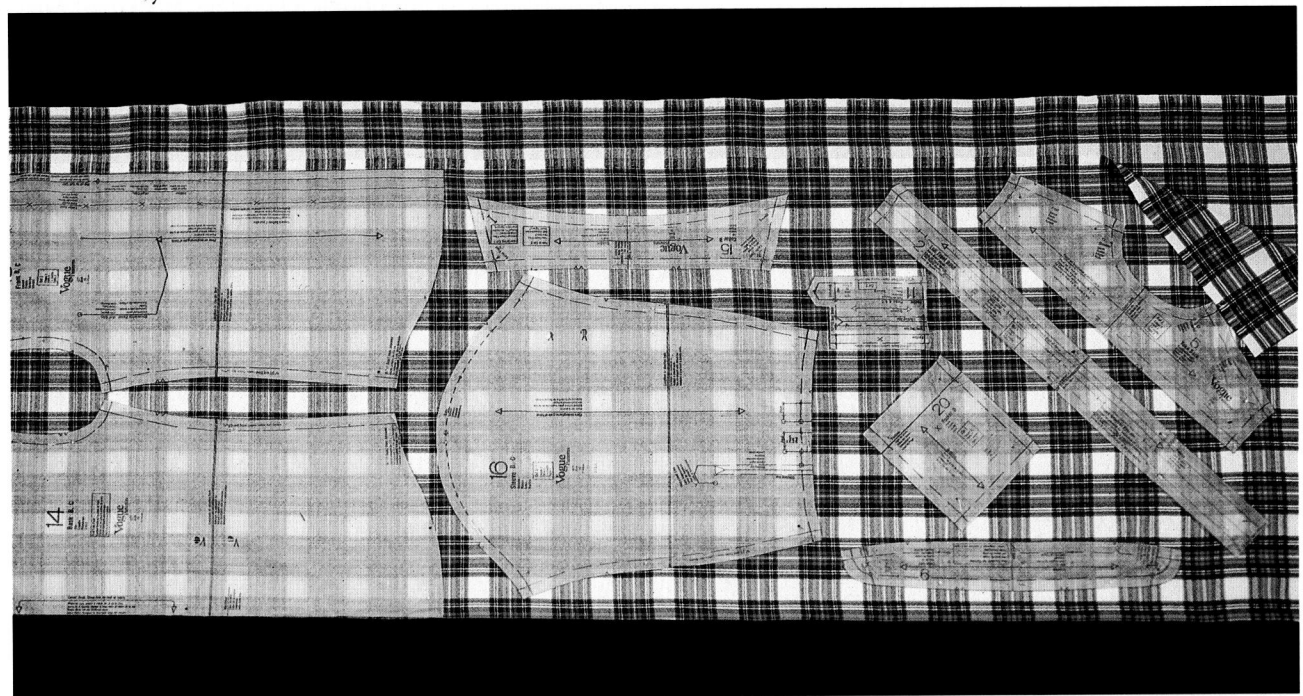

Fold fabric through center of repeat, lining up color bars to match on both fabric layers. Pin layers together to prevent shifting. Place most dominant color bar at center front and center back, or place centers in middle of plaid repeat. Lay out straight hemlines on complete, not partial, crosswise color bar. Lay out curved hemlines on least dominant color bar. Place yokes, pockets, and bands on the true bias.

How to Lay Out Uneven Plaids

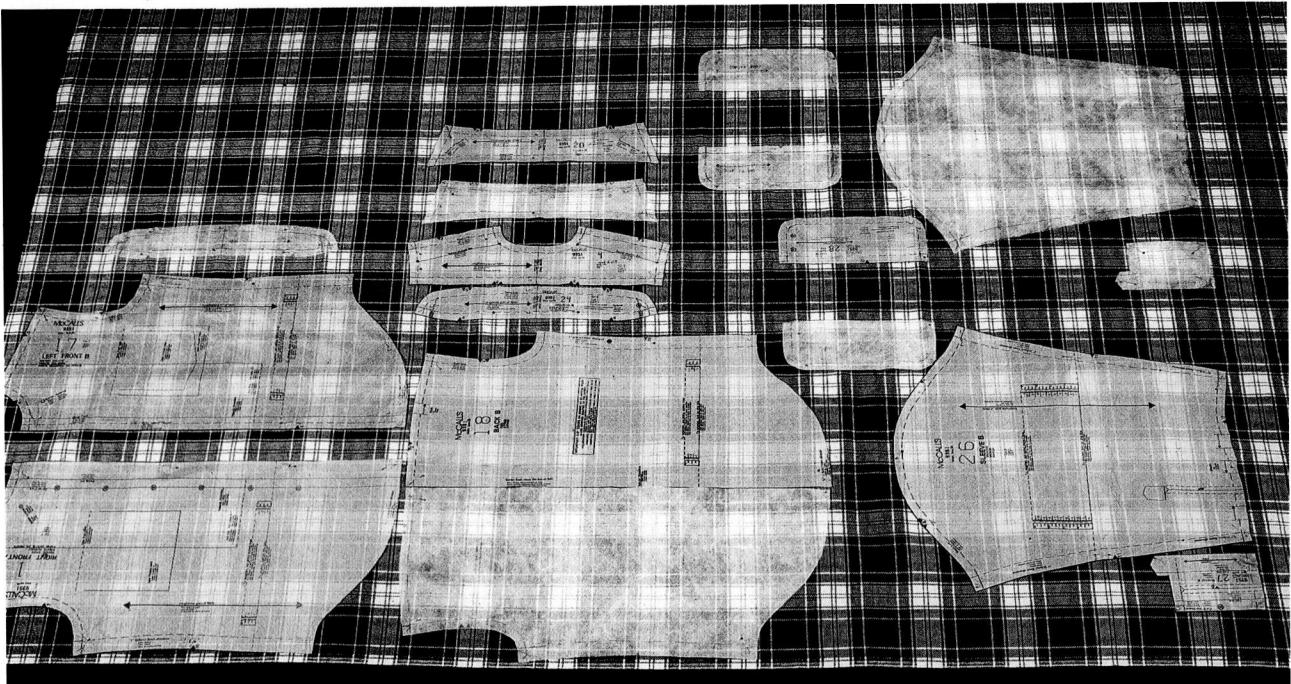

Lay out pattern on single layer of fabric, flipping pattern pieces over to cut right and left halves. Place most dominant color bar at center front and center back. Position hemlines as described above for even plaids. Optional layout method is folding fabric through dominant color bar and pinning all pattern pieces right side up. Place pattern pieces in one direction only, using "with nap" layout. Plaid will repeat around the garment instead of forming a mirror image on each side of the center front and center back seams.

How to Match Plaids

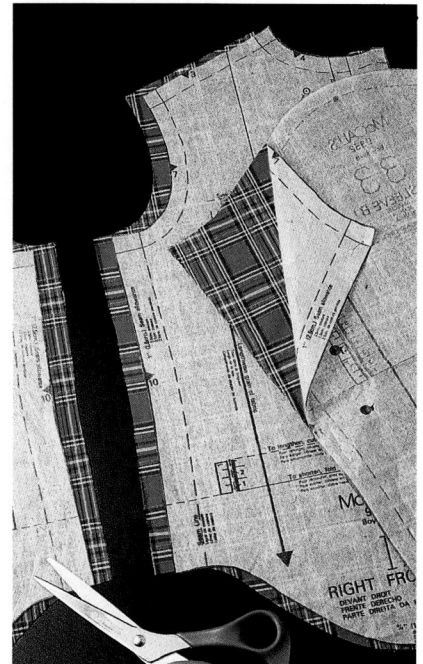

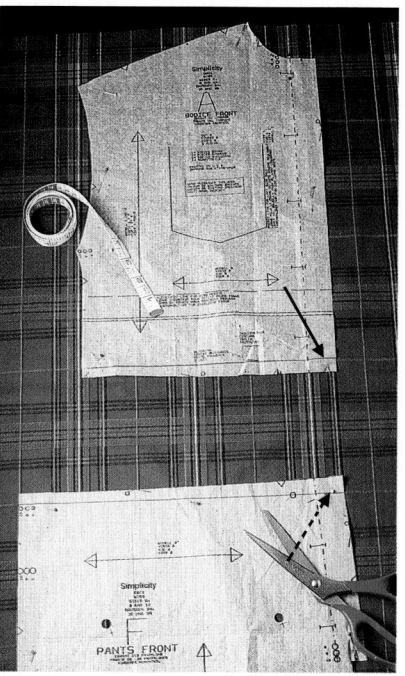

Match plaid at side seam notches of major front and back patterns. Lay out sleeve pattern so plaid matches at front armhole notch. Always match plaids at seamlines, not cutting lines.

Duplicate position of plaid on garment front when laying out front facing pattern. Match center back of upper collar to center back of garment. Plaids may not match where collar joins front facing, but will look balanced side to side.

Position bodice, top, or jacket pattern on plaid. Overlap skirt pattern at hemline or seamline, and transfer matching plaid line (arrow). Align skirt marking on same plaid line (broken arrow). For separates, make sure plaid on jacket hem matches at lap line on skirt.

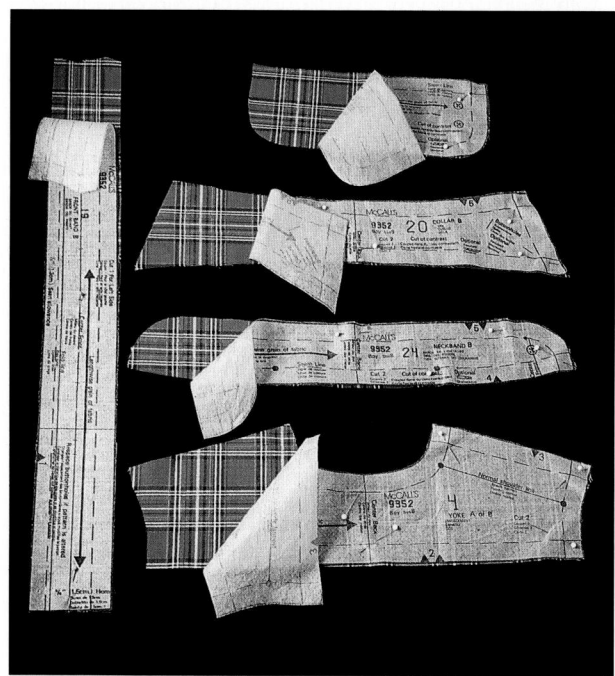

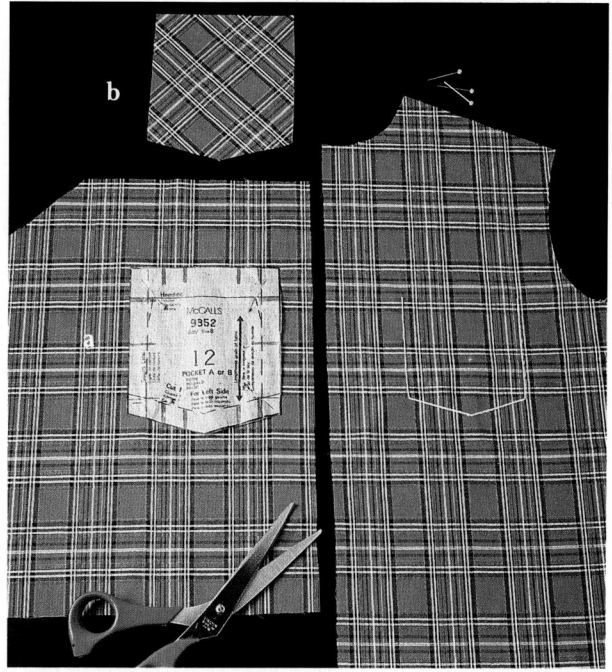

Align yoke, cuff, waistband, and other straight-edged pattern pieces so seamlines, not cutting lines, fall on complete color bar. If there is enough fabric, position these pieces on dominant color bar for attractive accents.

Trace plaid from garment section to patch pocket pattern to duplicate plaid placement when laying out pocket. Perfectly matched pocket (a) will blend into overall plaid. Pocket can also be cut on true bias grain (b) as accent.

How to Lay Out Even Stripes

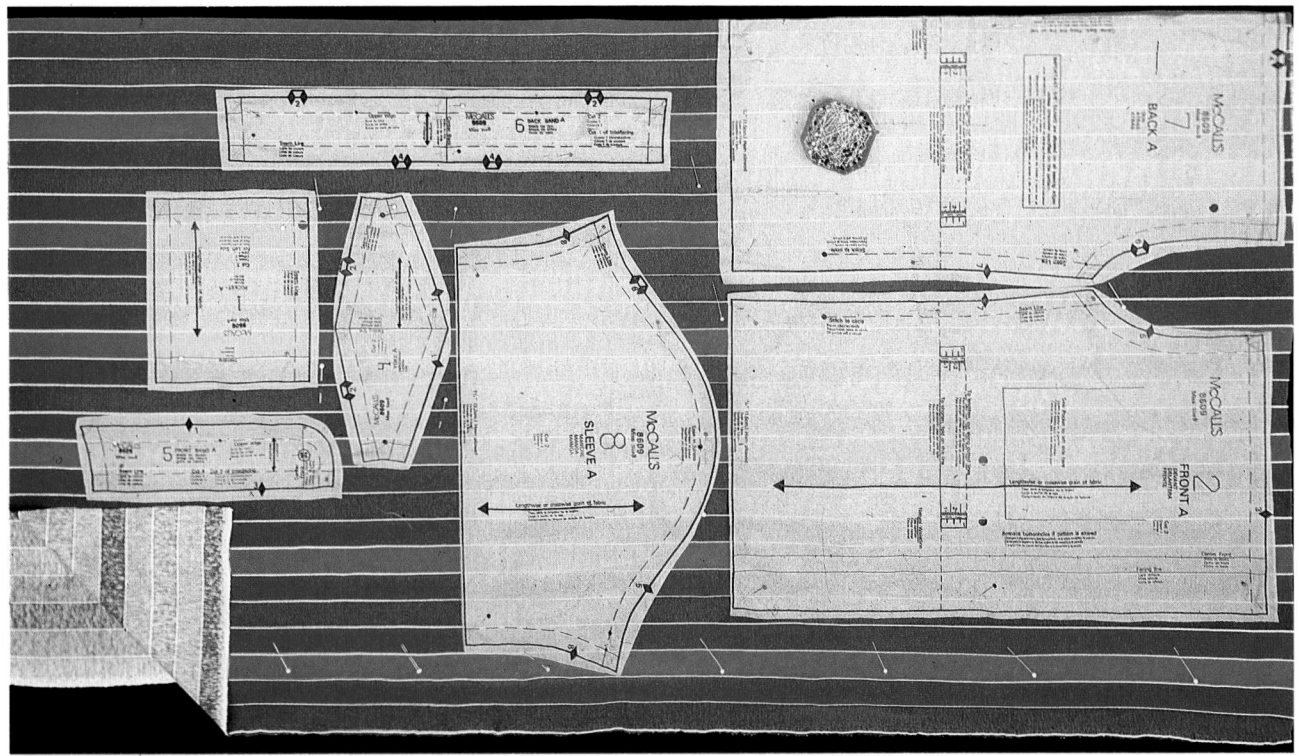

Fold fabric through center of repeat. Stripes should match perfectly on both layers. Pin to prevent fabric from shifting during layout. Cut details, such as pockets and applied bands, so stripes contrast with direction of main garment sections if desired.

How to Lay Out Uneven Stripes

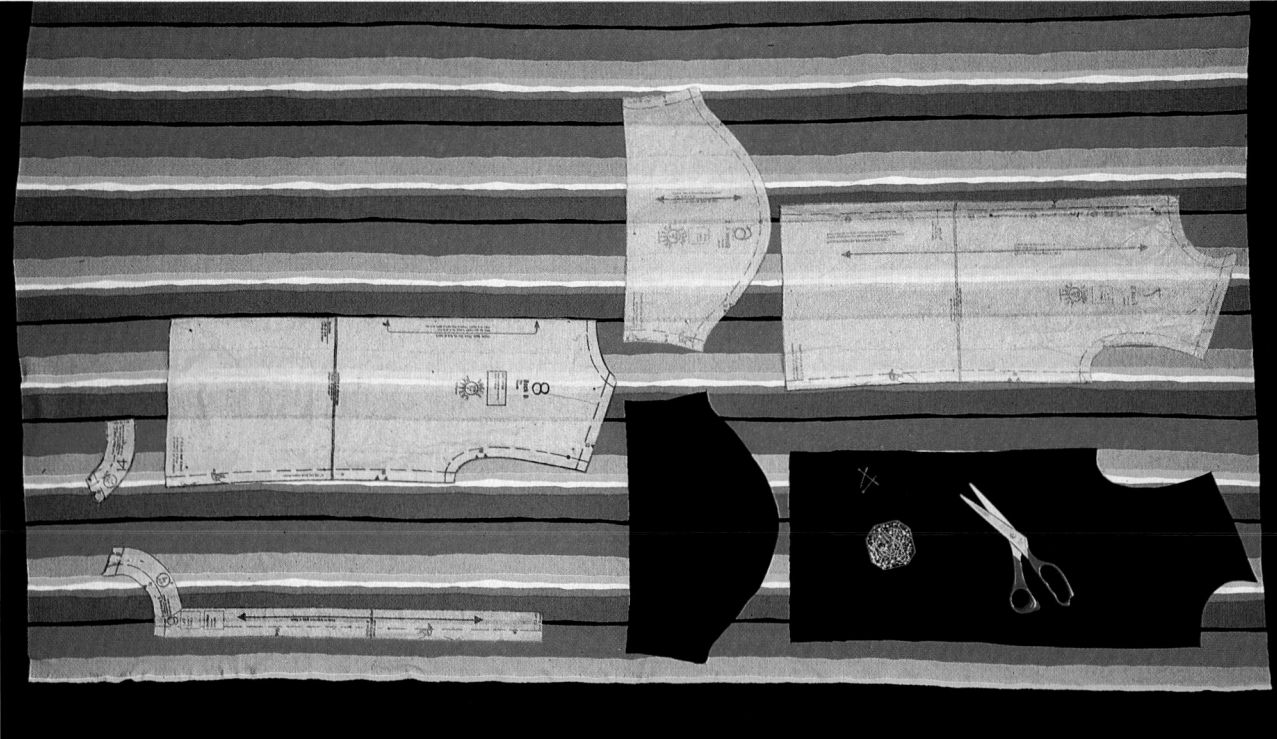

Lay out pattern on single layer of fabric, and flip pattern pieces over to cut right and left sides. For balanced look, place dominant stripe at center front and center back. Use "with nap" layout so stripes encircle garment. Position straight-edged pieces so complete, not partial, stripe falls along seamline.

How to Match Uneven Stripes at a Front Closing

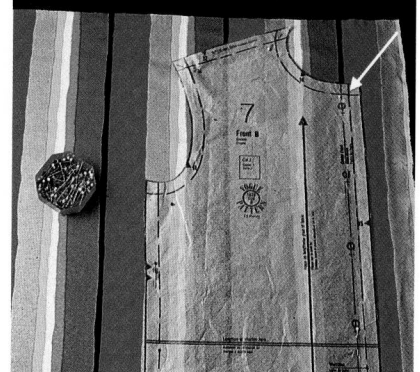

1) Pin pattern to single layer of fabric, placing pattern so center front (arrow) falls on dominant stripe. Squint or stand back from fabric to pick out this stripe if it is not immediately apparent.

2) Flip pattern over to cut out other side front. Position center front of pattern (arrow) on same dominant stripe as in step 1, left.

3) Sequence of stripes in repeat continues across both garment sections. Dominant stripe is in center front.

Keeping Plaids and Stripes Matched during Sewing

Pin. Place pins through edges of color bars. Color bars are easy to see on wrong side of fabric if design is woven. Be sure pins penetrate same edge of color bar on both fabric layers. Pin at frequent intervals. Stitch with Even Feed™ foot.

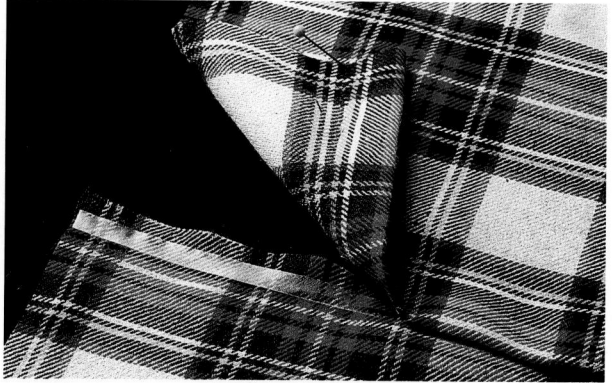

Double-faced basting tape. Place tape next to one seamline, on right side of fabric. Fold back seam allowance of adjoining garment section to match plaid or stripe. Stitch seam; then remove basting tape from seam allowance.

Slip-baste. 1) Press seam allowance under on one edge. Lap folded edge over seam allowance of adjoining section, matching stripes; pin at right angles to fold.

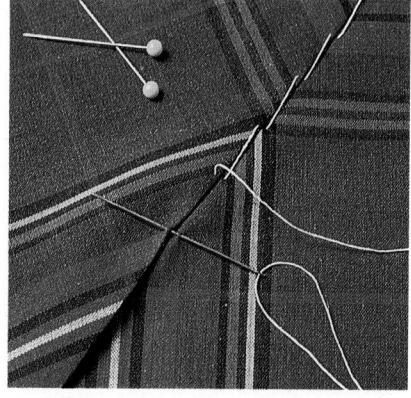

2) Bring needle up through three layers of fabric and out at fold on right side of garment. Take a tiny stitch below first stitch through single layer and through the fold.

3) Remove pins, and fold out seam allowance. From inside, machine-stitch through center of small stitches formed under folded edge. Remove basting.

Fabulous Fakes

Synthetic Fur, Suede & Leather

Synthetic fur has a deep pile texture on the right side, which can imitate the coloring and texture of natural pelts, such as mink **(1)**, seal **(2)**, fox **(3)**, or sheepskin **(4)**. Or a synthetic fur fabric can have a novelty texture **(5)** that looks man-made. Synthetic furs are usually made from modacrylic or polyester fibers and can be washed and dried by machine. Most have a knitted backing.

Synthetic suede is a nonwoven, softly napped polyester/polyurethane fabric that closely resembles genuine sueded leather. Unlike real leather, it is an easy-care fabric that can be washed and dried by machine. The main difference between synthetic suedes is weight. Lightweight synthetic suedes **(6)** drape softly and do not require special patterns. Mediumweight types **(7)** are more like real suede.

With conventional sewing methods, you may need to take extra finishing steps, such as fusing the seam allowances and topstitching the edges because suedes are difficult to press flat with conventional pressing techniques. Or you can use flat construction techniques, such as lapped seams and faced hems. Besides solid colors, the synthetic suedes can be embossed **(8)** or printed **(9)** to add textural interest.

Synthetic leather/vinyl fabrics can be smooth **(10)** or textured **(11)**. Like suedes, vinyls have different weights. Lightweight, supple vinyls have a knitted or woven backing. When handling vinyls, use many of the same methods used for synthetic suedes, except vinyls are damaged by heat and steam so they cannot be pressed.

Guide to Sewing Synthetic Fur, Suede & Leather

Equipment & Techniques	Synthetic Fur	Synthetic Suede	Synthetic Leather/Vinyl
Machine Needles	Size 14 (90) or 16 (100)	Size 11 (75); 16 (100) for topstitching/buttonhole twist	Size 11 (75)
Stitch Length	10 to 12 per inch (2.5 cm)	8 to 10 per inch (2.5 cm)	8 to 10 per inch (2.5 cm)
Millimeter Stitch Setting	3 to 2.5	3.5 to 3	3.5 to 3
Thread	All-purpose polyester or polyester/cotton; topstitching/buttonhole twist or two strands of all-purpose for topstitching.		
Interfacings	Omit	Fusible	Sew-in
Special Seams	Butted	Lapped, topstitched, welt	Topstitched, welt
Special Hems	Faced or lined to the edge	Topstitched, faced, fused	Topstitched

Techniques for Synthetic Fur

The same kinds of garments furriers create from luxury pelts can be sewn from synthetic fur: coats, jackets, vests, and capes with simple seams and a loose fit. Synthetic fur can also be used for details on a garment, such as the collar or hood lining on a coat or jacket. Because synthetic furs are bulky, avoid details such as pleats, gathers, darts, and patch pockets. Replace buttonholes with alternative closures such as loops, snaps, or hooks and eyes.

Layout, Cutting & Marking

Simplify the pattern wherever possible. Lap the seamlines of the front facing and jacket front, for example, to cut the facing in one with the body of the garment. Omit interfacing pattern pieces; synthetic furs rarely need this extra strength and support. Cut inner garment sections, such as in-seam pockets or a back neckline facing, from coat lining fabric to reduce bulk. Undercollars can be cut from the fur fabric, lining, or synthetic suede.

For easier handling, trim off the extra tissue margins from the pattern pieces on the cutting lines if using a plain seam. Trim the pattern on the seamlines for butted seams (opposite).

Lay out the pattern on a single layer of fabric, backing side up, and use a "with nap" layout. If using fabric that looks like real fur, run the pile down toward the hem of the garment. For a natural look, balance and match color shadings on the major pattern pieces. Novelty furs can be cut with the nap running up, down, or across the garment.

Use long pins with large plastic heads to hold the pattern on the backing; long, quilting, or super pins work well. Cut through the backing only, using the tips of shears or a single-edged razor blade or blade cutting tool. Avoid cutting into the pile on the right side. Transfer pattern markings to the backing of cutout garment sections, using pins and chalk or marking pen.

Pressing

Rarely do synthetic furs need pressing; steam can be damaging to the pile. Usually you can smooth seams and garment edges into place with your fingers. A soft, rolled edge is more appropriate on these fabrics than a sharp crease. To renew flattened pile, tumble the garment in a clothes dryer.

Two Ways to Cut Synthetic Fur

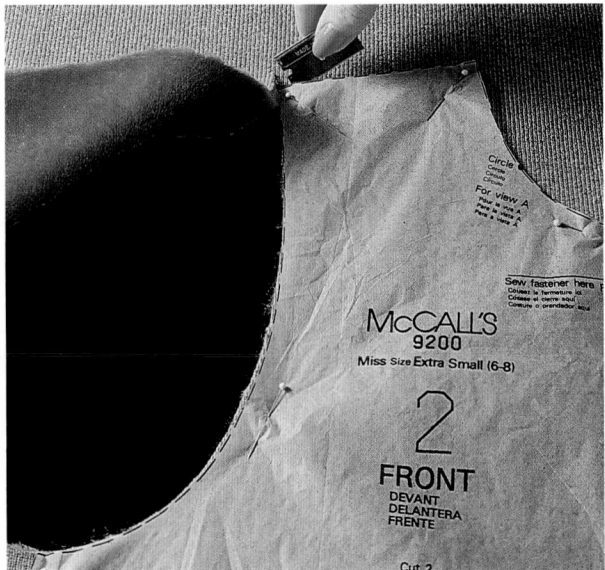

Single-edged razor blade makes clean, quick cuts without damaging pile on right side. Hobby knife can also be used to cut synthetic fur.

Shears can be used to cut synthetic fur, using tips to snip through backing alone. Shears must be sharp and close at tips for successful cutting.

Seams

Because synthetic furs are bulky, adjust your sewing machine pressure and tension for straight and zigzag sewing. Use fabric scraps to test the stitch, decreasing the pressure on the presser foot and loosening the needle tension until the stitch is balanced. For even feeding of the layers, smooth the pile away from the raw edges and stitch in the direction of the nap.

For long-haired synthetic furs with a knit backing, the butted seam is ideal. It resembles the seam used by furriers and joins garment sections with minimum bulk. Butted seams can be used throughout the garment, even on enclosed seams at collars and facings. For synthetic furs with shallow pile, you can use a plain seam. To reduce bulk, shear the pile from the seam allowances after stitching.

How to Sew a Butted Seam on Synthetic Fur

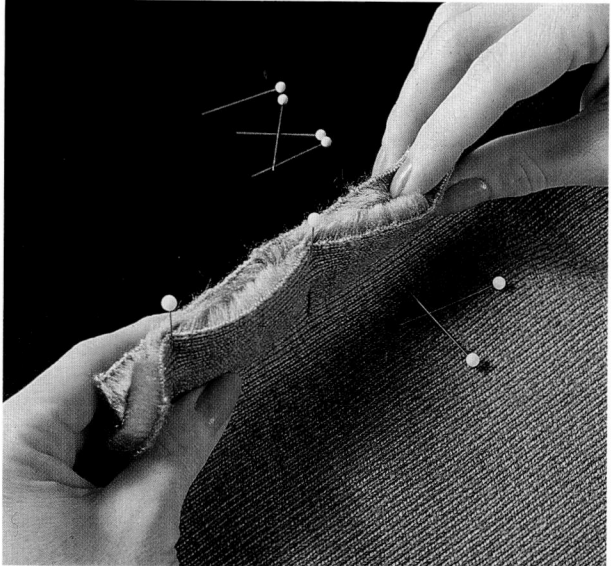

1) Brush pile away from raw edges to make them easier to handle when sewing. Pin seam with raw edges together. (Pattern pieces have been cut out on the seamline.)

2) Stitch with short, wide zigzag stitch. Position fabric so needle swings past cut edges on right-hand side. Or use 2-thread flatlock seam on the serger.

3) Open out both layers, and pull them gently apart until cut edges meet. Seam should lie flat with slight ridge along stitches.

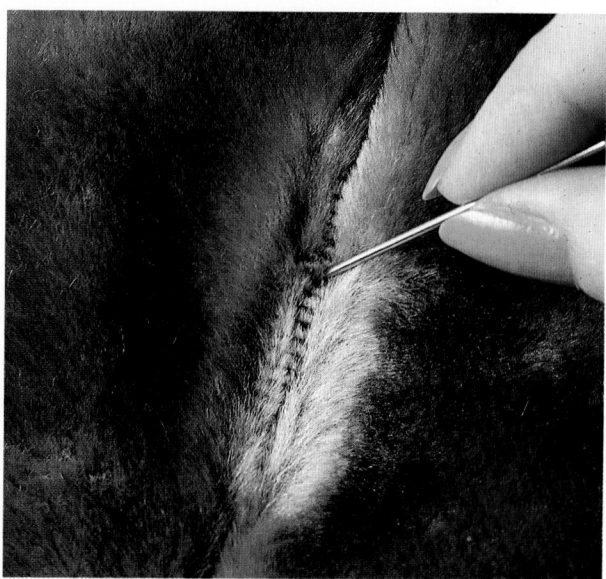

4) Lift out pile caught in seam, using T-pin or blunt tapestry needle and working from right side. Finished seam is barely visible.

Hems

Put in hems by hand, using a catchstitch between the hem and the garment. Smooth the finished hem with your hands, but do not try to press it with an iron. A soft edge is more attractive on synthetic furs than a flat, pressed edge. For bulky furs, face the hem with lining fabric to reduce bulk, or use a double row of catchstitching to support a regular turned-up hem.

How to Sew a Faced Hem

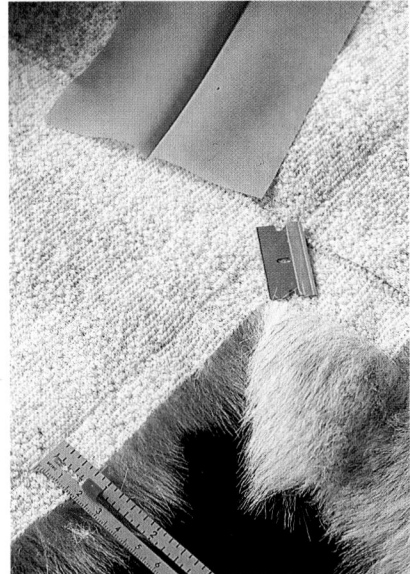

1) Trim hem allowance to ¾" (2 cm). Cut 4" (10 cm) wide bias strip of coat lining fabric for hem facing; press in half lengthwise.

2) Stitch folded facing strip to hem, raw edges together, in ¼" (6 mm) seam. Use pin or tapestry needle to free pile caught in seam.

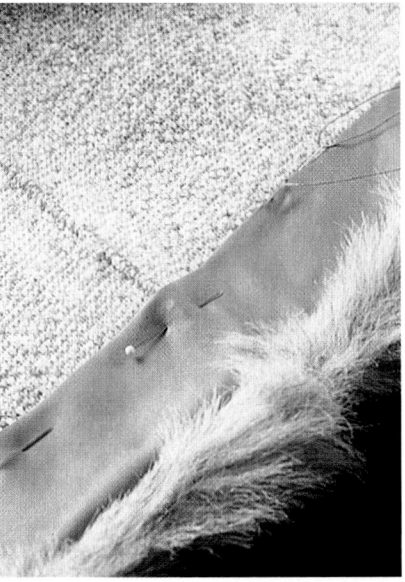

3) Turn facing to inside of garment with ½" (1.3 cm) of synthetic fur above hem. Slipstitch upper edge of facing to fur backing.

How to Sew a Double-stitched Hem

1) Finish raw edge of synthetic fur by trimming evenly, then zigzag stitching. Position zigzag stitching so it overcasts raw edge.

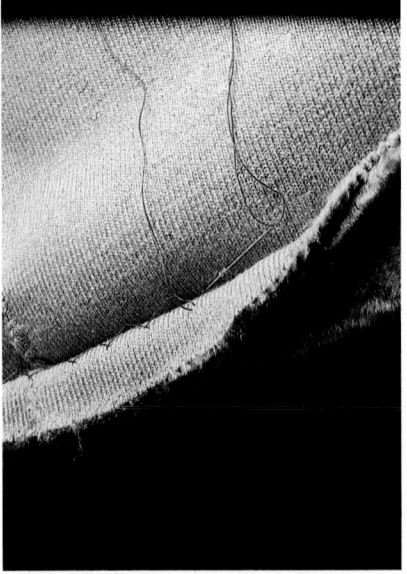

2) Turn hem up and baste at half-way point. Fold hem down along basting. Loosely catchstitch hem to backing, using heavy-duty thread or buttonhole twist.

3) Fold hem up; then fold back hem edge to sew another row of catchstitches between finished hem edge and fur backing.

Closures

Selection of a closure on fake furs depends on the length of the pile. Avoid zipper and buttonhole closures on long-haired fake furs. Use an alternative closure, such as fur hooks and eyes, silk-covered snaps, or crocheted loops with buttons. Sew buttons on with heavy-duty thread, doubled and coated with beeswax.

To insert a zipper in short-pile fur, use an exposed technique to prevent the pile from catching in the zipper teeth.

On front closings, loops can substitute for buttonholes. Crochet chainstitched loops; anchor first stitch in knit backing. Then use buttons with metal shanks, or make thread shanks for sew-through buttons.

Closures for Synthetic Fur

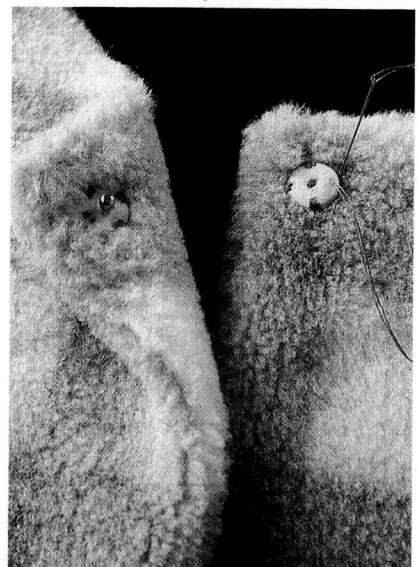

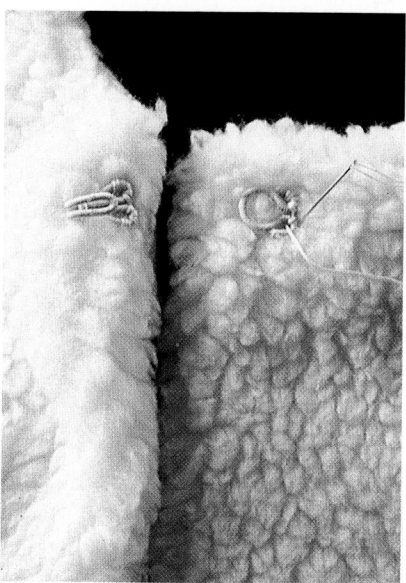

Silk-covered snaps, covered with black, brown, white, beige, or gray lining fabric, can be used instead of buttons and buttonholes.

Fur hooks and eyes, covered with lustrous thread, may be used on fur coats and jackets. One set at waistline and one at neckline are usually all you need.

Zippers are inserted in short-pile fabrics with teeth exposed. Use plastic sport zipper. Shear pile from overlapping seam allowance to eliminate bulk. Slipstitch zipper tape to backing.

Techniques for Synthetic Suede

Although there are patterns that include separate directions for handling synthetic suede, any pattern can be adapted for synthetic suede techniques. To make sewing easier, look for styling that suits the characteristics of the fabric. Mediumweight synthetic suede drapes stiffly and does not ease well, making it most suitable for pattern silhouettes that are loosely fitted and boxy in shape. Nearly any softly draped or fitted fashion is appropriate for light-weight suede fabrics. Keep in mind that topstitching is usually used on seams and on edges to keep them flat; topstitching may affect the drape of the pattern.

Sewing Methods

Before laying out the pattern, decide the sewing method that you will use because it determines how to cut and how much fabric is needed. Choose between *conventional* sewing techniques, *flat* construction methods, or a combination of both.

Conventional sewing techniques use traditional ⅝" (1.5 cm) seam allowances. These methods can be used exclusively throughout a synthetic suede garment if desired.

Flat construction methods require modification of the layout. For a lapped seam, trim the seam allowance from one side of the seam. Before cutting, determine the finished length and eliminate the hem allowance. Flat construction methods are usually combined with conventional sewing techniques.

Whether using conventional sewing techniques or flat construction methods on a garment, use conventional seams for set-in sleeves. You may need to modify set-in sleeve patterns by removing some of the ease at the sleeve cap. Raglan, dolman, and kimono sleeve styles are easier to sew.

Making a Test Garment

Before purchasing synthetic suede, test the pattern fit by sewing it in a fabric with similar drape, such as felt, denim, or heavyweight nonwoven interfacing. Use a test garment to determine finished hem and sleeve lengths. Transfer fitting changes to the pattern pieces. This gives you confidence that the garment will fit and you will not have to rip out seams. Equally important, you can use the adjusted pattern to make a trial layout and determine exactly how much fabric to purchase.

Layout Considerations

Synthetic suede does not shrink and needs no special preparation before layout. Preshrink fusible interfacings by soaking them in warm water for 10 minutes. Roll in a towel to remove excess moisture, and then hang or lay flat to air dry.

Unlike woven or knit fabrics, synthetic suede does not have a grain, but it does have a nap. Use a "with nap" layout so all pattern pieces are placed in the same direction. Because it does not have a grain, you can reduce the amount of fabric needed by turning the pattern pieces slightly so they fit together like a jigsaw puzzle. The pattern pieces can be tilted up to 45° without affecting color shading in the finished garment. Nap may be reversed to create a color variation for collars and cuffs.

When using flat construction, trim the seam allowance from the lapped side of the seam to reduce the amount of fabric that will be needed. Place straight edges of pattern pieces on the straight edge of the fabric.

Cutting, Marking & Stitching

Place pattern pieces on a single layer for cutting. Use sharp shears or rotary cutter for cleanly trimmed edges. To save fabric, be careful not to cut beyond the edge of the pattern. After cutting, label the wrong side of each garment section with chalk or a piece of masking tape to eliminate confusion between the right and wrong sides later.

Transfer pattern markings to the wrong side of cutout sections with washable marking pen or chalk. To mark on the right side, apply transparent tape to the suede and mark the tape with pencil or marking pen. Remove the tape as soon as possible. Chalk can also be used on the right side of the fabric, but always test the chalk on a fabric scrap to be sure the chalk lines can be removed. When using lapped seams, mark seamlines on the right side of underlapping garment sections.

Synthetic suede tends to shift when sewn, so extra care is necessary for successful stitching. To prevent shifting, it is important to hold the fabric layers together securely by preparing seams with basting tape, glue stick, or fusible web. Use taut sewing, silicone lubricant, the Even Feed™ foot, or roller foot to help the fabric feed evenly.

Pressing

Synthetic suede is difficult to press to a sharp crease, and traditional pressing methods do not apply. To apply fusible web, steam synthetic suede with a hand steamer, or hold a steam iron just above the surface. Pressing on the right side can damage the nap. Press on the wrong side, using a press cloth and synthetic setting. As an added precaution against flattening the nap, press it face down on a piece of self-fabric. If the napped texture inadvertently becomes flattened, brush with a toothbrush or terry towel. When it is necessary to press on the right side, use a wool press cloth. Use a wooden clapper to flatten edges and force steam into the fabric.

How to Lay Out a Pattern on Synthetic Suede

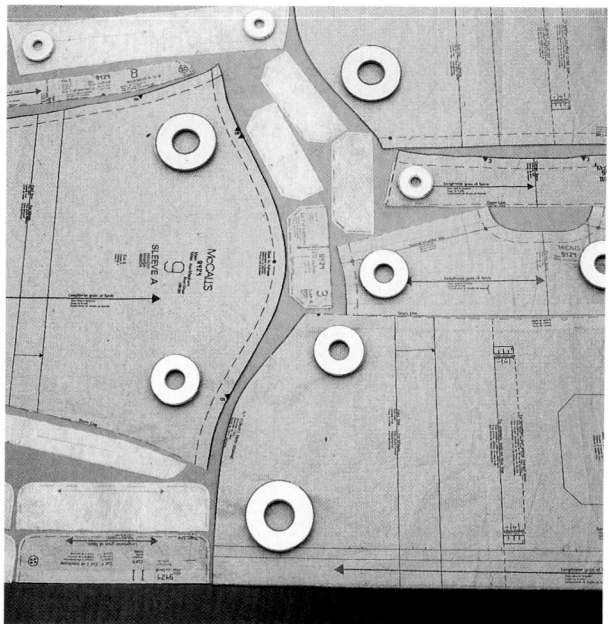

Choose between conventional and flat sewing techniques. Conventional method **(a)** uses standard pattern directions, and fabric is handled like most woven fabrics. Flat method **(b)** uses lapped seams, so one seam allowance may be trimmed before cutting. Hems and facings may be eliminated.

Use "with nap" layout, with all pattern pieces laid out in the same direction. For flat method, trim seam allowances from one side of lapped seams. Place straight edges on straight edge of fabric. Tilt pattern pieces up to 45° because synthetic suede has no grain. Butt pattern pieces to save fabric because it does not ravel. Test layout before buying fabric because you may be able to buy less than pattern calls for.

How to Remove Ease from a Set-in Sleeve Pattern

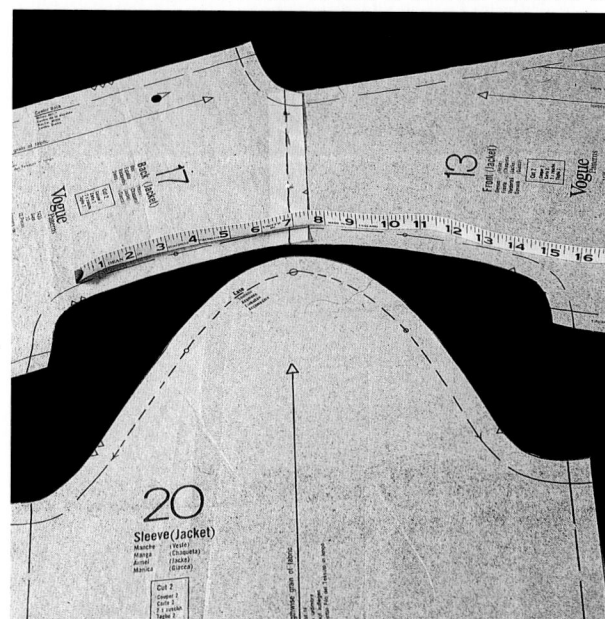

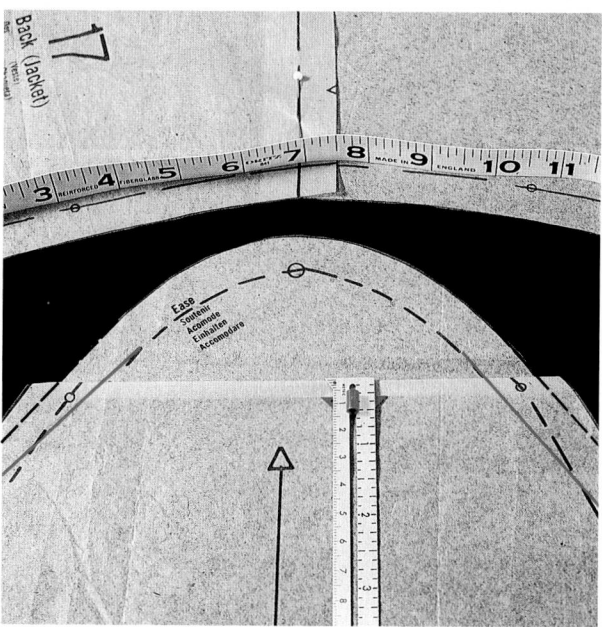

1) Stand tape measure on edge to measure seamline of pattern at sleeve cap and armhole. Measure between front and back notches on both pieces. Compare measurements to determine amount of ease in sleeve cap. Remove ease from sleeve if there is more than 1" (2.5 cm) difference.

2) Draw a line 2" (5 cm) below top of sleeve cap, and fold a tuck on line to remove excess ease; leave total of 1" (2.5 cm) ease in sleeve cap. The depth of the tuck equals one-fourth of total amount to be removed. [If removing 1" (2.5 cm) of ease, make tuck ¼" (6 mm) deep.] Straighten cutting line.

Conventional Techniques

Conventional method includes welt, topstitched, and plain seams. Seam allowances for this method are standard ⅝" (1.5 cm). Use plain seams for set-in sleeves, for curved seams, such as pants crotch, and for tubular sections, such as sleeves.

Collar and front facings use the standard ⅝" (1.5 cm) seam allowances. Trim and grade seams carefully to prevent rippling. To keep enclosed seams crisp and neat, topstitch or edgestitch.

Hem is turned up and fused in place; topstitching is optional. Because synthetic suede eases poorly, use turned up hem on straight hemline only.

Zippers can be inserted using lapped or centered method when conventional seams are used.

Conventional Construction

Topstitched seam has seam allowances that lie flat. Seams on synthetic suede are not easily pressed open, so topstitching or fusing may be used to hold seam allowances in place.

Bound buttonhole is made with window openings in garment and facing; it is not necessary to turn under raw edges. Lips are folded and fused.

Patch pocket is cut with standard ⅝" (1.5 cm) seam allowances and lined to edge. Topstitching keeps pocket edges crisp and neat.

Flat Techniques

Flat method uses lapped seams. Seam allowance on bottom layer (underlap) is full ⅝" (1.5 cm); on the top layer (overlap), entire seam allowance is omitted. Before pattern layout, decide which seams to lap and the direction of the lap.

Collar and front facings require ⅛" (3 mm) seam allowances. Trim edge on seamline after layers have been topstitched together. This technique works because synthetic suede does not ravel or fray.

Shaped hem and curved edges use self-fabric facing strip cut to match curve of garment edge. Fuse and topstitch in place.

Zipper is inserted in lapped seam. Trim upper seam allowance during pattern layout. Trim lower seam allowance to ⅛" (3 mm) to reduce bulk before inserting zipper.

Flat Construction

Lapped seam requires planning to determine direction of lap. Generally vertical seams, such as side seams, lap front to back; details, such as collars, cuffs, and waistbands, lap over major garment section.

Slash buttonhole uses a stitched rectangular window around the buttonhole opening. Fusible web between garment and facing keeps fabric layers together. Method also works on vinyl and other nonwoven fabrics.

Patch pocket is cut without seam allowances. Open edge has narrow faced hem. Apply pocket to garment with narrow strip of fusible web, then edgestitch or topstitch.

Stitching Tips for Synthetic Suede

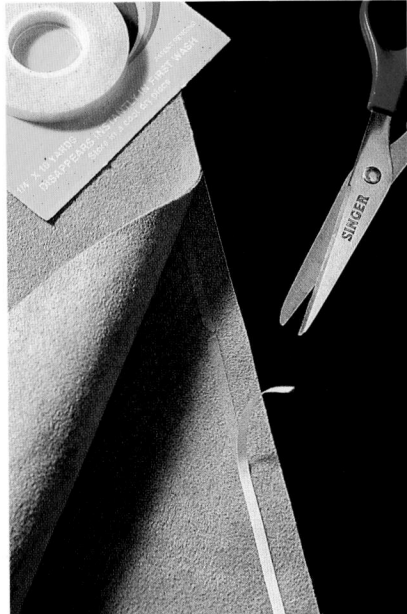

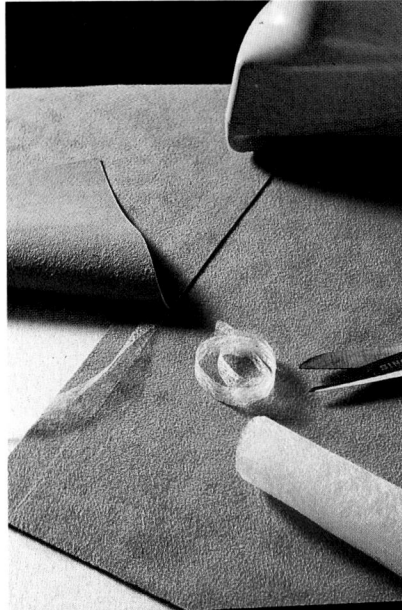

Basting tape can be used to prepare seams for stitching. Use short pieces, about 12" (30.5 cm) long. Finger press tape ⅛" (3 mm) from seamline, remove the tape backing, and place other fabric layer on top. Do not stitch through tape. Remove tape after stitching if it is not water soluble.

Fusible web, cut in scant ¼" (6 mm) strips, can be used to prepare lapped seams for stitching. Lay web strip on underlapping seam allowance, next to seamline, and steam lightly. Position overlapping fabric, and steam lightly again to fuse layers together. Layers do not have to be permanently fused.

Glue stick can be used to prepare seams or edges for sewing. Apply lightly in seam allowances; then press fabric layers together. Glue stick applies best when refrigerated. It holds temporarily, yet layers can be peeled apart before it dries completely. Glue dissolves when garment is washed.

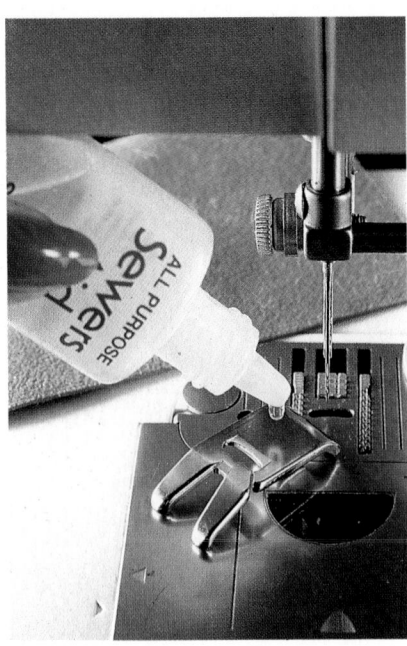

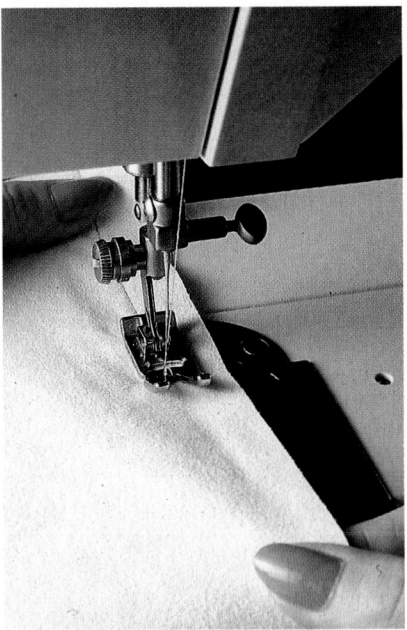

Silicone lubricant makes synthetic suede easier to sew. Add one drop of lubricant to spool of thread before filling bobbin and threading machine needle. Also apply to needle, bottom of presser foot, and throat plate.

Taut sewing helps control the way synthetic suede feeds through sewing machine. Place fingers in front of and behind presser foot to hold fabric layers securely. Do not pull or force fabric; this can bend needle or cause uneven stitches.

Even Feed™ **foot (a)** feeds top and bottom layers of fabric together. Roller foot **(b)** is a universal accessory with small rollers that help the fabric feed evenly through the machine.

Conventional Seams on Synthetic Suede

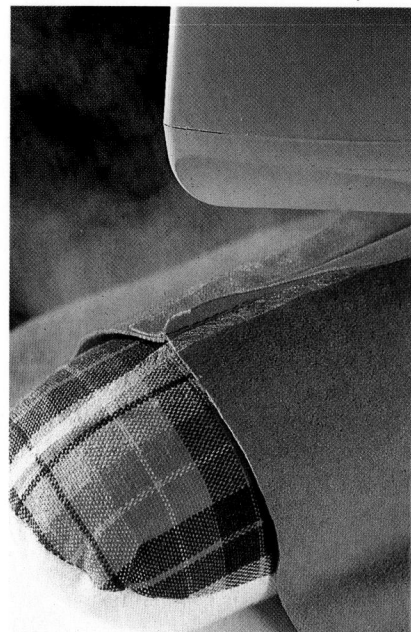

Plain seam. Stitch ⅝" (1.3 cm) seam; press open. Steam and pound with clapper. To hold seam flat, fuse scant ¼" (6 mm) wide strip of fusible web under each seam allowance. Steam over seam roll to fuse.

Topstitched plain seam. Use all-purpose sewing thread for topstitching that blends into the nap. To highlight topstitching, use buttonhole twist.

Welt seam. Finger press both seam allowances to one side. Trim inner seam allowance to just under ¼" (6 mm). Topstitch ¼" to ½" (6 mm to 1.3 cm) from seamline.

How to Sew a Lapped Seam

1) Mark seamline on right side of underlapping garment section with chalk dots or tape. Do *not* mark right side with marking pen without testing to see that ink can be removed. (Seam allowance of overlapping section has already been removed.)

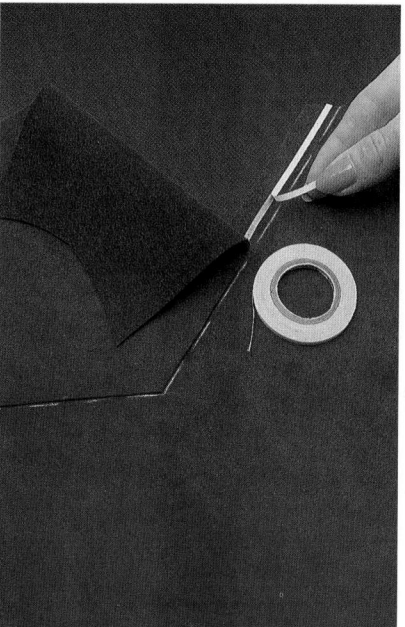

2) Place basting tape ⅛" (3 mm) from marked seamline. Use 12" (30.5 cm) strips for easy handling. Remove paper backing. Overlap adjoining section, and finger press to hold. Use fusible web or glue stick instead of tape, if desired.

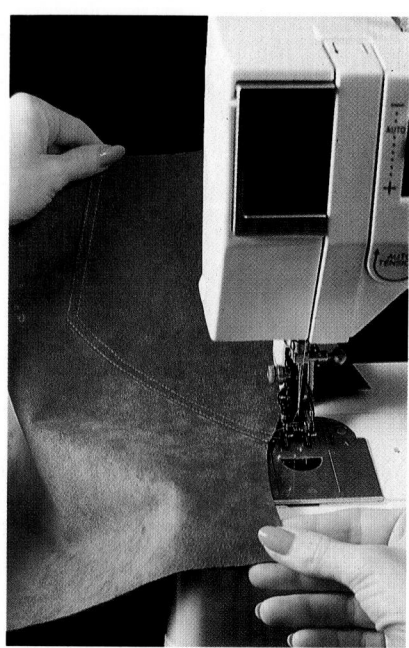

3) Edgestitch from right side along cut edge of overlapping garment section. Remove basting tape if it is not water soluble. Then topstitch ¼" (6 mm) from cut edge. Finished seam looks like flat-fell seam and lies flat without bulk.

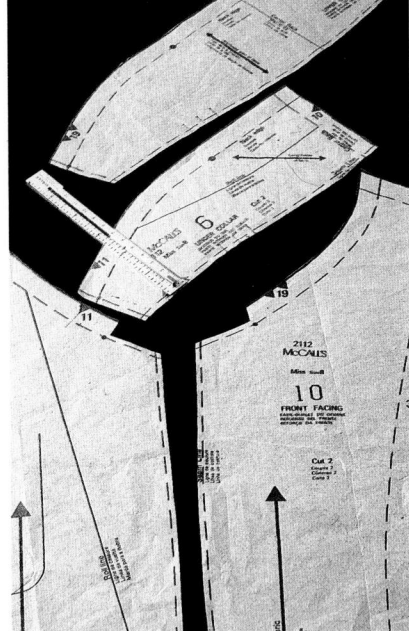

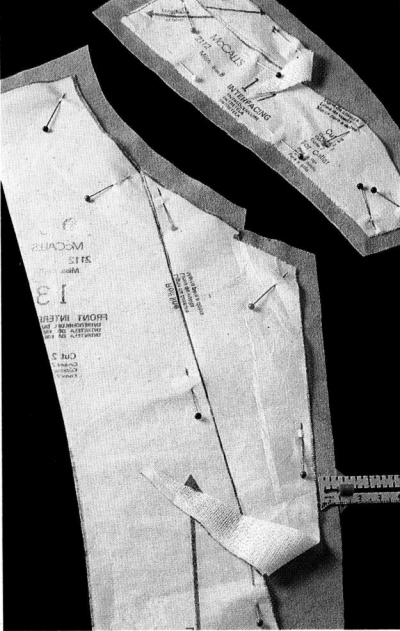

1) Reduce seam allowances to ⅛" (3 mm) on outer edges of collar and facing patterns. Use standard ⅝" (1.5 cm) seam allowance for conventional seam at neckline. Lay out pattern, and cut garment sections using adjusted patterns.

2) Cut interfacing ¼" (6 mm) inside seamline on outer edges. Cut fusible interfacings smaller than garment sections so the interfacing will not show between layers on finished garment edges. Slash interfacing at lapel roll line to form hinge.

3) Mark seamlines on wrong sides of undercollar and front facing to help position interfacing correctly. Fuse interfacing to undercollar and front facing, positioning interfacing ⅜" (1 cm) from outer edges. Stitch upper collar to front facings in ⅝" (1.5 cm) seam.

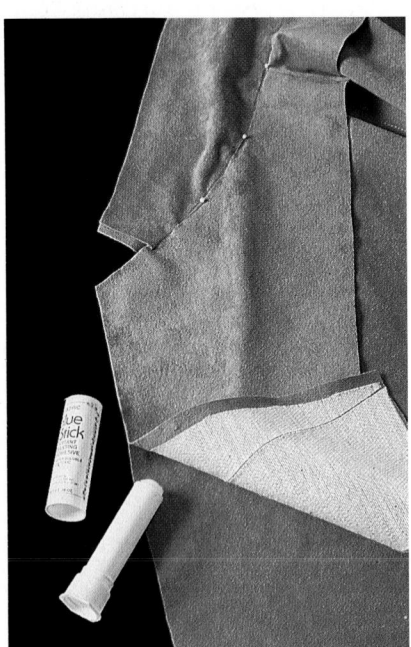

4) Baste wrong side of collar and front facing to garment, using glue stick. Be careful to line up outside edges evenly at front facing. Undercollar edge may extend slightly beyond collar if necessary for smooth roll.

5) Edgestitch scant ¼" (6 mm) from outer edges of collar and front facing. Topstitch ¼" (6 mm) from edge-stitching. Select same thread used for sewing lapped or topstitched seams on previous garment sections.

6) Trim edges next to edgestitching. Use rotary cutter or sharp shears and even strokes for clean-cut edges. Collar and lapel edges lie flat without bulk from enclosed seam allowances.

How to Face a Hem or Edge

1) Cut ¾" (2 cm) wide facing to match shape of garment edge. Grainline and nap of facing are not important, so scraps can be used without waste. Piece facing if necessary by butting cut edges.

2) Fuse the butted edges to a small rectangle of lightweight lining fabric with ½" (1.3 cm) wide strips of fusible web. Zigzag edges together.

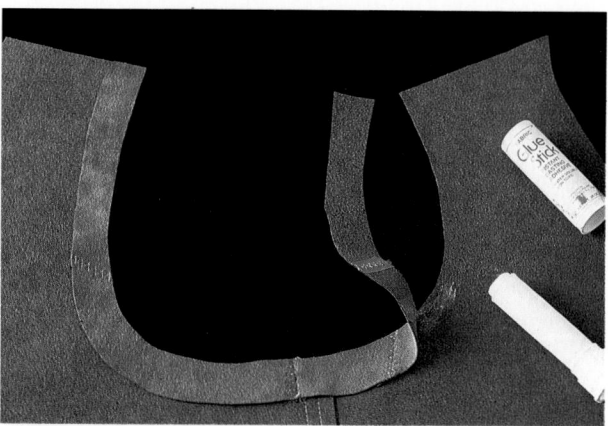

3) Baste facing to garment, wrong sides together, using basting tape or glue stick. Facing could also be fused to garment with strips of fusible web.

4) Edgestitch scant ¼" (6 mm) from cut edges; then topstitch ¼" (6 mm) from edgestitching. Stitch from right side of garment. Trim both fabric layers next to edgestitching.

How to Make a Straight Hem

1) Steam hem fold, working from inside of garment. Pound with clapper for sharp edge. Fuse hem in place, using ¼" (6 mm) strip of fusible web placed ¼" (6 mm) below cut edge of hem.

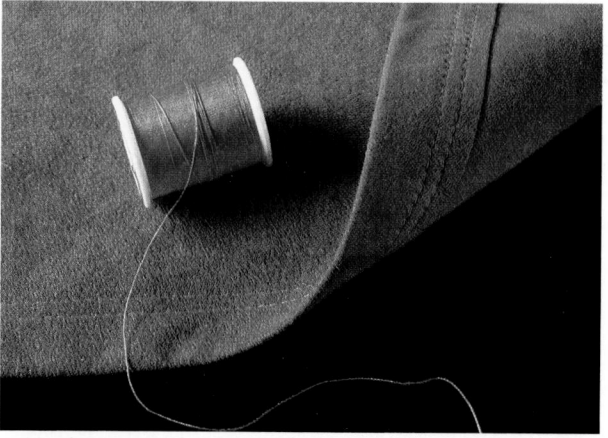

2) Topstitch hem, if desired, using longer stitches with buttonhole twist or two strands of all-purpose thread. Add second row for detail. Use folded hem on straight hemline only.

Closures

Zippered or buttoned closures are commonly used on synthetic suede. Finishing the edges of the closure is simple; synthetic suede does not ravel, so it is not necessary to fold under the cut edges.

On lightweight suede, use traditional zipper insertion methods for lapped or centered application. For extra body, a narrow self-fabric facing is used on the lap side of a lapped zipper. For centered application, the zipper can be inserted in a conventional seam (below). You may also include a facing on both sides of the zipper, using the flat facing technique as for a lapped zipper.

For the quickest method to make buttonholes, stitch a narrow rectangle around the buttonhole and slash open. For a more tailored look, modify a traditional bound buttonhole with topstitching.

How to Insert a Centered Zipper in a Conventional Seam

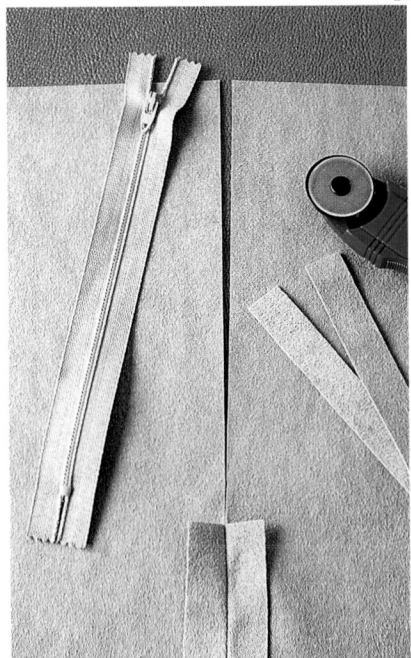

1) Trim off seam allowances in zipper placket area only.

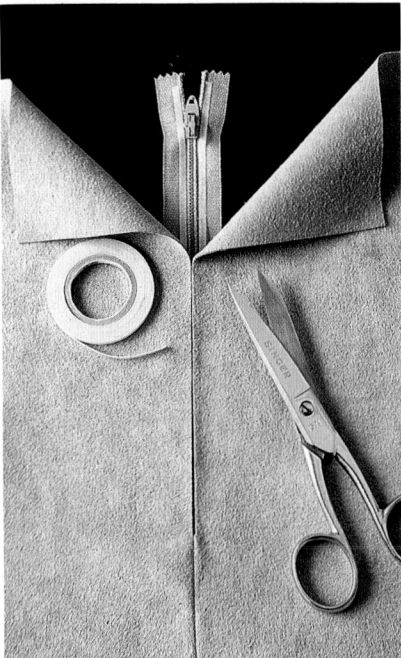

2) Tape or glue zipper to placket with cut edges meeting at center of zipper.

3) Center ½" (1.3 cm) transparent tape over zipper to use as stitching guide. Stitch zipper in place ¼" (6 mm) from each cut edge.

How to Insert a Zipper in a Lapped Seam

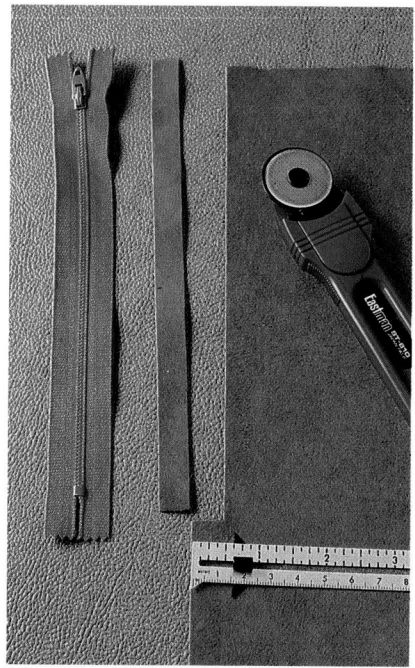

1) Trim seam allowance on underlap to ⅛" (3 mm) for length of zipper placket. (Seam allowance on overlap has already been removed for lapped seam.)

2) Baste underlap to zipper so cut edge lies next to zipper coil. Use basting tape or glue stick for basting. Edgestitch underlap to zipper tape.

3) Cut facing 1" (2.5 cm) wide and 1" (2.5 cm) longer than zipper opening. Baste facing to wrong side of overlap. Edgestitch the length of zipper placket; then topstitch ¼" (6 mm) from stitching.

4) Lap faced edge of zipper placket over zipper so faced edge covers edgestitching on underlap. Baste seam below zipper; stitch lapped seam (page 95) to meet stitching on placket.

5) Fold garment sections with right sides together to expose facing. Baste free side of zipper to this facing, and stitch.

6) Fuse facing to garment with ¼" (6 mm) strip of fusible web.

How to Make a Bound Buttonhole in Synthetic Suede

1) Cut window in right side of garment for each buttonhole. Window is ¼" (6 mm) wide and desired length of buttonhole. Cut two rectangles 1½" (3.8 cm) wide and 1" (2.5 cm) longer than buttonhole.

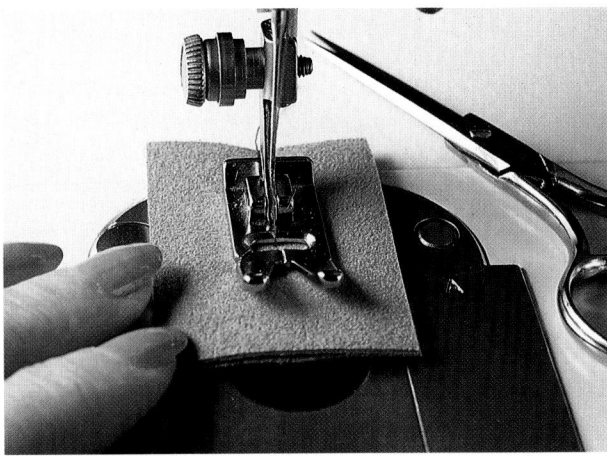

2) Bastestitch two self-fabric rectangles through center with right sides together for buttonhole lips.

3) Press wrong sides of rectangles together. Use glue stick or a ⅛" (3 mm) strip of fusible web inside folds to hold layers together.

4) Center lips over buttonhole window on wrong side. Glue or fuse in place. Grade excess fabric from edges of lips to reduce bulk. Attach facing.

5) Edgestitch around buttonhole window, stitching through all layers.

6) Cut matching window in garment facing to finish buttonhole. Remove bastestitching.

How to Make a Slash Buttonhole

1) Use glue stick or fusible web between garment and facing at each buttonhole location. Finger press or steam to fuse two fabric layers together.

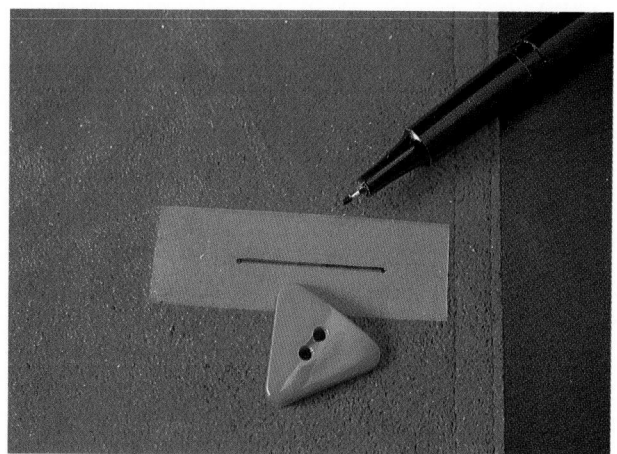

2) Mark exact length of buttonhole on piece of transparent tape applied to right side of garment at each buttonhole location.

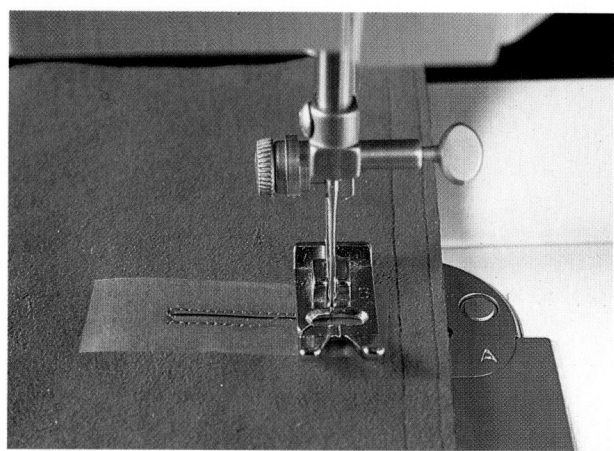

3) Stitch 1/16" (2 mm) from buttonhole marking, using 14 stitches per inch (2.5 cm). Reinforce ends of buttonhole by backstitching.

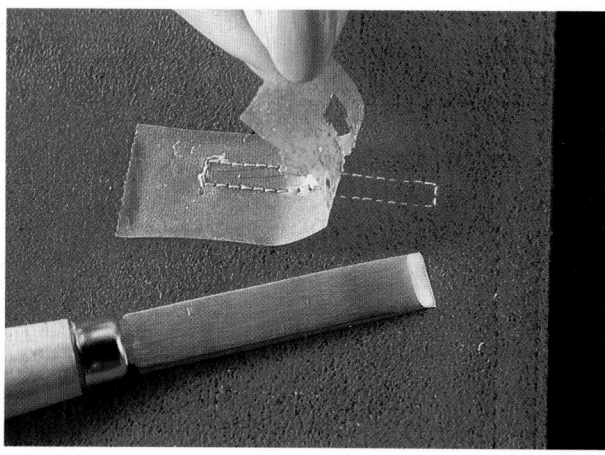

4) Remove tape, and cut buttonhole open with razor blade or buttonhole cutting tool.

How to Reinforce Buttons

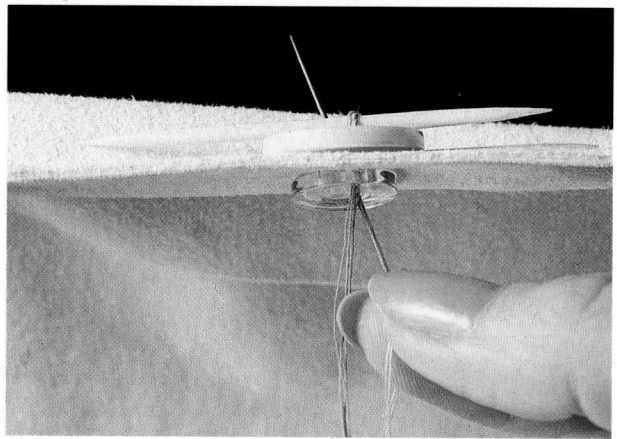

1) Use small, flat reinforcement button on inside of garment to prevent outside button from tearing fabric. Sew through both buttons at same time.

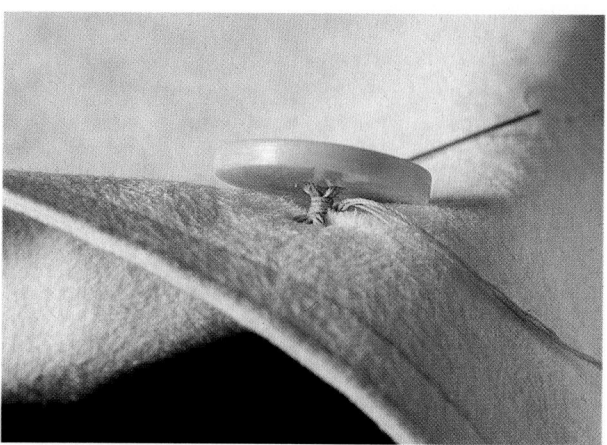

2) Make thread shank at least 1/4" (6 mm) long on outside button. Shank accommodates thickness of fabric at faced closings.

Techniques for Vinyl

Leather-grained vinyl is a less expensive alternative to real leather. It has the look and texture of leather but does not breathe and give as leather does. The waterproof characteristics of vinyl make it ideal for outer wear and rainwear.

Some techniques for sewing vinyl fabric are similar to sewing synthetic suede. Like synthetic suede, vinyl has no grainline and does not drape well. You may want to make a test garment and trial layout. You may also remove the ease from a set-in sleeve pattern as for synthetic suede (page 91).

Not all synthetic suede techniques are practical for vinyl. Because vinyl fabrics have a knit backing, the lapped method of sewing does not apply. In addition, vinyl has no nap or surface texture unless it is embossed to resemble leather. To prevent waste, you can devise a pattern layout that fits the pieces together in jigsaw-puzzle style. Pins leave holes in vinyl, so baste with tape, glue stick, or paper clips.

Like pins, stitches leave permanent holes, and short stitches weaken the vinyl surface. Do not backstitch to start or finish a line of stitching; instead, tie the threads or use liquid fray preventer to seal the threads. If using the bound or slash buttonhole methods given for synthetic suede on pages 100 and 101, lengthen the stitch to 8 to 10 per inch (2.5 cm) on vinyl. Use a longer, wider-spaced zigzag stitch for machine-made buttonholes. Interface button and buttonhole areas with patches of woven sew-in interfacing. Or eliminate buttonholes altogether and use alternative closures such as zippers or snaps.

If vinyl does not feed smoothly for topstitching, use silicone lubricant on the throat plate and presser foot, or cover the throat plate with strips of tissue or tear-away paper. For stitching, use an Even Feed™ foot or a roller foot on your sewing machine and the technique of taut sewing. Vinyl dulls machine needles quickly, so plan to insert a new needle frequently.

Vinyl is easily damaged by heat, so use topstitching instead of pressing to keep seams and edges flat. Do not use fusible products. If interfacing is needed, use a sew-in type.

Special Techniques for Handling Vinyl

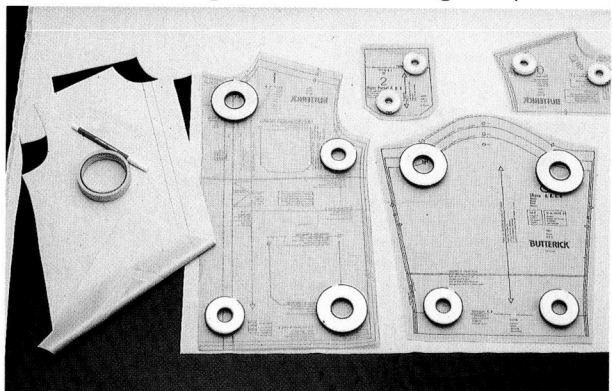

Lay out pattern on single layer of vinyl. Use weights to hold pattern in position for cutting; pins leave holes. Mark backing with chalk or marking pen. Mark vinyl surface with transparent tape.

Topstitch hems. Keep hem narrow to avoid puckers on curved edges because vinyl eases poorly. Use long stitches, 8 to 10 per inch (2.5 cm) for topstitching. Use tape to hold hem in place.

Seams

Plain seam should be topstitched open, rather than pressed. Do not press vinyl; heat causes permanent damage.

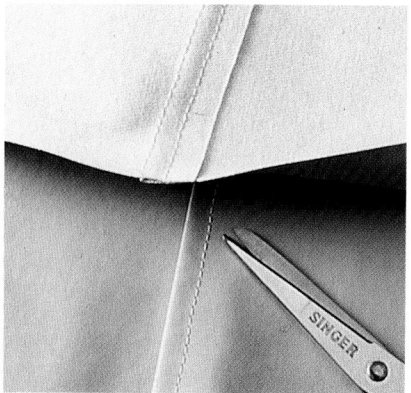

Welt seam requires one row of topstitching. Smooth both seam allowances to one side, and trim enclosed seam allowance before topstitching the seam.

Flat-fell seam encloses all raw edges and requires two rows of topstitching. Use on vinyl with brushed tricot backing for comfortable unlined jackets.

Closures

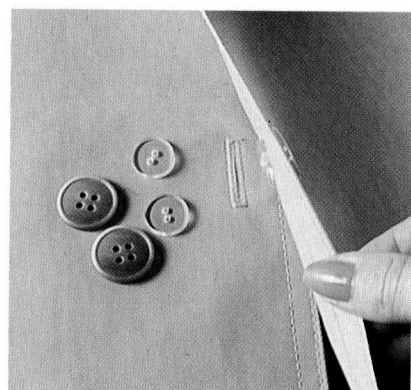

Buttons require small, flat reinforcement buttons inside garment to prevent ripping. Use machine-made, slash, or bound buttonholes on vinyl.

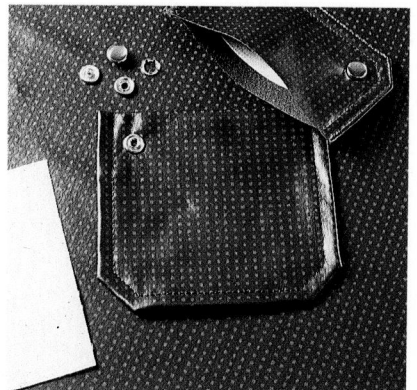

Gripper snaps make excellent substitutes for buttons and buttonholes. Before applying snaps, slip interfacing or twill tape between vinyl layers as reinforcement.

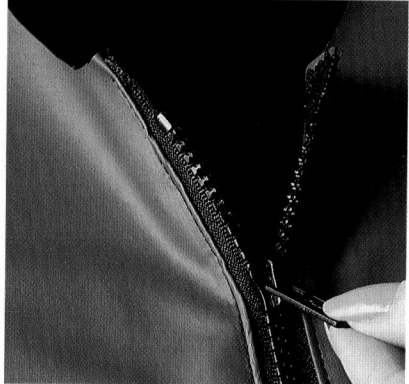

Zippers with large plastic teeth are often used on jackets. Use insertion method that exposes zipper teeth; contrasting zipper is decorative.

Knits

Knits

A knit is a fabric made from interlocking looped stitches. Because of this construction, knits shed wrinkles well, are comfortable to wear, and are easy to sew because they do not ravel. There are many kinds of knits, and most of those available for sewing can be grouped into five general categories.

Firm, stable knits do not stretch significantly and are handled similarly to woven fabrics. In this group are double knits **(1)**, which have fine lengthwise ribs on both sides. It is difficult to tell the right and wrong side of a double knit unless the right side has a decorative design. Raschel knit **(2)** is a lacy or open knit texture that does not stretch because lengthwise threads are locked into some of the knitted loops. Some raschel knits are made from bulky yarns and look like bouclé wovens or hand knits. Others are made from finer yarns and look crocheted.

Lightweight single knits have fine ribs running lengthwise on the right side and loops running crosswise on the wrong side. Pull the crosswise edge of a single knit and it will roll to the right side. Single knits such as jersey **(3)**, tricot **(4)**, and interlock **(5)** do not stretch lengthwise, but they do have crosswise give.

Textured knits may be single or double knits. This category is distinguished by a surface texture, usually on the right side. Knitted terry **(6)** and velour **(7)** are pile knits that look like their woven namesakes; however, they usually have a great deal of crosswise stretch. Also in the category of textured knits are sweater knits **(8)**. Patterned sweater knits have floats on the wrong side where colored yarns are carried from one motif to another. This limits their crosswise stretch. Comfortable sweatshirt fleece **(9)** looks like a single knit on the right side; the wrong side has a soft, brushed surface. It is usually fairly stable with little stretch in either direction.

Two-way stretch knits have a great degree of stretch crosswise and lengthwise and a high percentage of resilient spandex fibers. Absorbent cotton/spandex and cotton/polyester/spandex knits **(10)** are favored for active sportswear such as leotards, body suits, and aerobic exercise outfits. Strong nylon/spandex knits **(11)** are resilient, even when wet, and are usually selected for swimwear.

Ribbing is a very stretchy knit that can be used for tops and for finishing knit garments at wrists, ankles, neck, and waist. One type is tubular ribbing **(12)**, which is sold by the inch (2.5 cm) and must be cut open along one lengthwise rib for sewing. Another type is rib trim **(13)**, which is color coordinated with sweater knits; one edge is prefinished, and the other is sewn to the garment.

Techniques for Knits

Patterns for knits depend on the stretch characteristics and weight of the knit. The list of suggested fabrics on the back of a pattern envelope usually includes a combination of knit and woven fabrics. If a knit is soft and lightweight, such as jersey, it is suitable for patterns that have gathers, draping, and similar features. If it is firm, such as double knit, a pattern with tailoring or a shaped, fitted silhouette is suitable. If it is bulky or textured, such as a sweater knit, a pattern with few seams and details works best to show off the knit texture.

Certain patterns, however, require knits that stretch. These are closely fitted pattern styles, such as swimsuits and leotards, which would be too small to wear if made from a fabric without elasticity, or tops and pants that use the knit for a comfortable close-to-the-body fit. Most patterns designed for knits have a stretch gauge printed on the back of the envelope. Test the knit that you have selected against the ruler gauge. When the pattern specifies "two-way stretch knit," test the crosswise and lengthwise stretchability of the knit.

Patterns designed for knits often have ¼" (6 mm) seam allowances. If the pattern you have selected has ⅝" (1.5 cm) seam allowances, trim them to ¼" (6 mm) when using knit sewing techniques.

Fabric Preparation

For best results, preshrink knits. Wash and dry them if they will be washed as part of their routine care. Use a bulk drycleaner if the finished garment will be drycleaned. It is not necessary to preshrink ribbing unless using a dark-colored ribbing on a light-colored garment.

If, after preshrinking, a knit still has a crease where it was folded on the bolt, steam the crease. If the crease cannot be removed by steaming, it is permanent. Refold the knit for pattern layout to prevent the crease from showing on the garment.

To straighten the ends of knits, draw a chalk line across the cut crosswise edges at right angles to the ribs. Cut the fabric on the chalk line.

How to Use a Stretch Knit Gauge

Correct knit for pattern stretches easily to right-hand side of the gauge printed on pattern envelope. To test, fold crosswise edge of knit over 3" to 4" (7.5 to 10 cm), and test fold against gauge. Knit that stretches even more than gauge requirements may still be used for pattern.

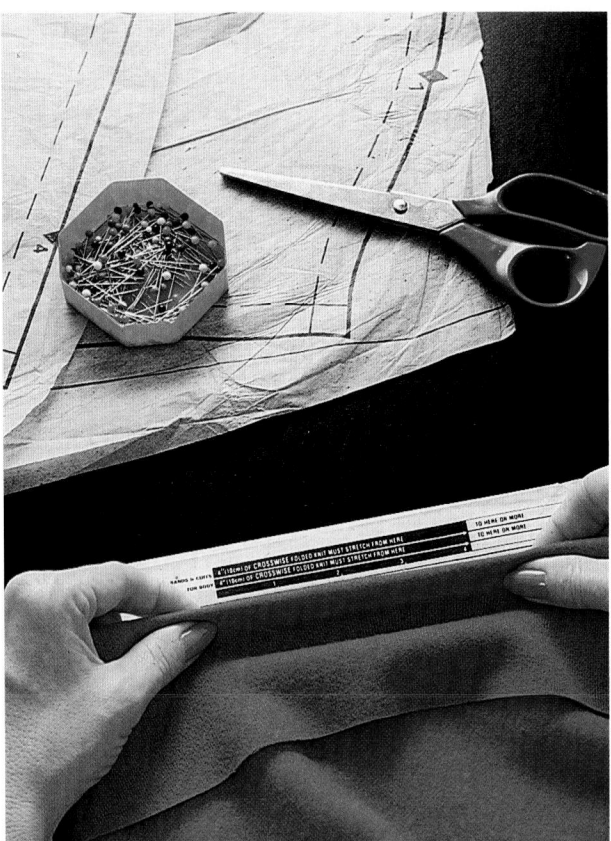

Wrong knit for pattern is forced beyond reasonable limits to satisfy gauge printed on pattern envelope. Ribs of knit are distorted, and stretched edge folds over on itself because of too much stress on fabric. Knit does not have enough natural elasticity for this pattern style.

Pressing

Press knits on the lengthwise ribs by lifting and lowering the iron. Use a low iron temperature setting, and raise the temperature as needed. Do not press across the ribs or handle the fabric until it is completely cooled. Either action can stretch knits out of shape.

Block sweater knits instead of pressing. To block, pat the fabric or the garment into shape on a flat surface. Steam with a hand steamer, or hold a steam iron above the knit surface. Allow the fabric to dry and cool completely before further handling.

Pattern Layout

Always use a "with nap" pattern layout on knits. Because of knit construction, they have a directional quality that shows up as a difference in color shading in the completed garment.

Stretch both crosswise edges of a knit before pattern layout to see if the knit runs. If so, the runs will occur more readily along one edge than the other. Position the run-prone edge at the garment hemline during pattern layout. The hem is subject to less stress, so the knit will be less likely to run after the garment is sewn.

When laying out and cutting a knit fabric, do not allow it to hang off the work surface. The weight of the fabric can distort the portion on the work surface, pulling it off-grain.

On bulky or textured knits, it is easier to lay out the pattern on a single layer of fabric. Position the textured side down; pin and mark on the smoother, wrong side of the knit. Use weights instead of pins on knits with open or lacy textures.

Interfacings

Interface knits to stabilize details, such as buttonholes, plackets, and patch pockets, and to support shaped areas such as collars. Select a supple interfacing that does not change the character of the knit. Two types of interfacings especially suitable for knits are fusible tricot and stretch nonwoven.

Tips for Interfacing Knits

Fusible tricot interfacing adds support and body to fashion knits without adding stiffness. It also allows for some crosswise stretch. Use tricot to stabilize detail areas such as cuffs, pockets, and plackets.

Stretch nonwoven interfacing stabilizes knit lengthwise but allows knit to stretch crosswise. Use this interfacing for flexible shaping in collars, necklines, facings, tabs, and zipper openings.

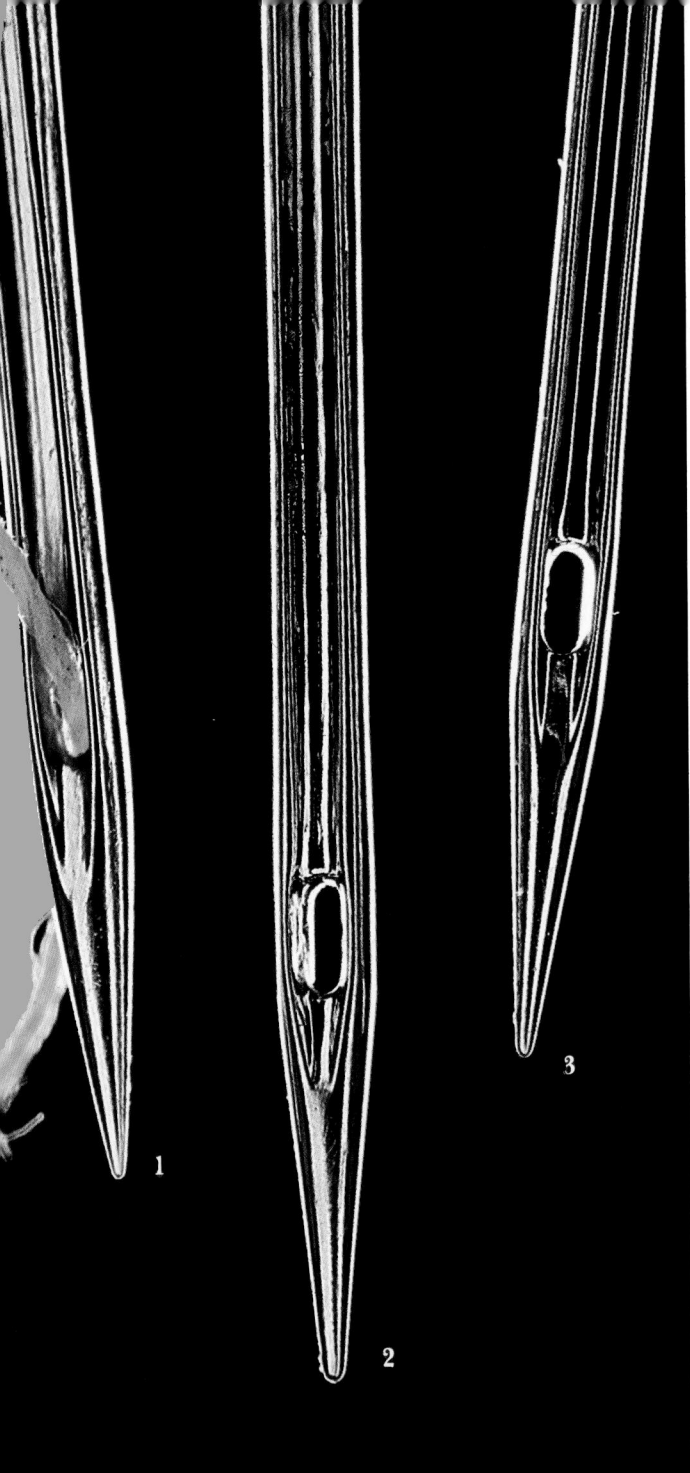

Selecting Needle, Stitch Length & Thread

For machine sewing, select needle size, stitch length, and thread type according to the weight of the fabric. The chart below suggests appropriate choices for lightweight, mediumweight, and bulky knits. For knits with a high percentage of synthetic fibers, such as nylon or polyester, change to a new needle midway through your sewing. Synthetic fibers cause extra wear on needle points and can dull them quickly.

Machine Needles for Knits

In addition to an appropriate needle size, select a needle type suitable for the knit fabric. There are three types of needles to consider. *Sharp point* needles **(1)**, the most common sewing machine needles, are most suitable for woven fabrics but can be used on knits with an open or loose texture. Sharp points are not suitable for firm, tight-knit textures or for knits made from strong polyester or nylon fibers. It is difficult for sharp points to pierce these knits. *Ballpoint* needles **(2)** penetrate knit fabrics by separating the yarns rather than piercing them. The tip of a ballpoint needle is rounded and blunt. Regardless of the knit, if the needle you are using snags the fabric, switching to a ballpoint needle may solve the problem. *Universal point* needles **(3)** are a modified ballpoint needle. The tip is less rounded and more tapered than that of a ballpoint needle. Universal points can be used on many fabrics, woven or knit. If skipped stitches are a problem, switching to a universal point needle may solve the problem.

Knit Guide for Needle, Stitch Length & Thread

Equipment & Techniques	Lightweight	Mediumweight	Bulky
Machine Needle Sizes and Types	Size 9 (70) or 11 (80) Ballpoint or universal	Size 14 (90) Ballpoint or universal	Size 14 (90) Ballpoint or universal
Stitch Length	12 to 16 per inch (2.5 cm)	9 to 12 per inch (2.5 cm)	9 to 12 per inch (2.5 cm)
Millimeter Stitch Setting	2.5 to 2	3 to 2.5	3 to 2.5
Thread	Extra-fine polyester or polyester/cotton.	All-purpose polyester or polyester/cotton.	All-purpose polyester or polyester/cotton.

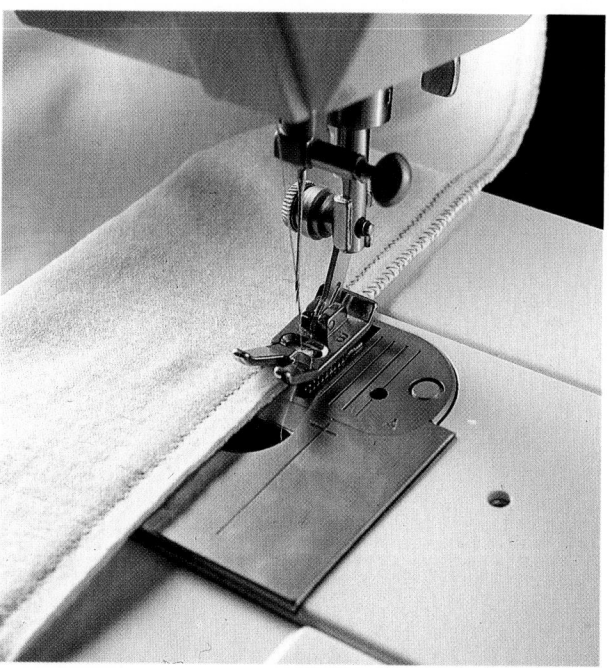

Stretch as you sew. When straight-stitching, build elasticity into seams by stretching fabric as you sew. Hold knit behind presser foot with left hand. Use right hand in front. Allow fabric to feed as it is stretched. Do not *pull* it through, which may break the needle and damage the fabric.

Zigzag seam. Use narrow zigzag stitch to sew seam, stretching slightly as you sew. Trim seam allowance to ¼" (6 mm). To reinforce, sew seam allowances together with zigzag or 3-step zigzag. This also prevents raw edges from curling on single knits, such as jersey and tricot.

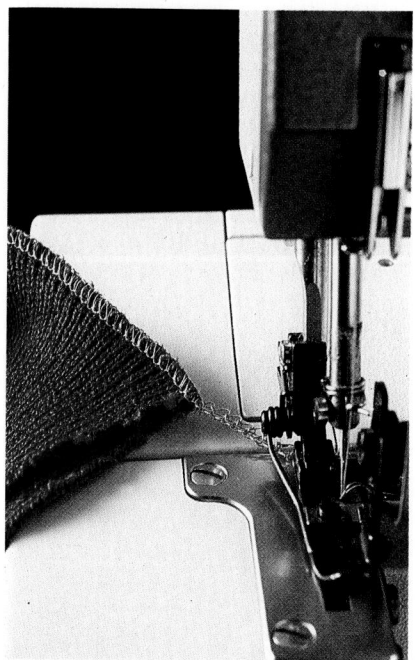

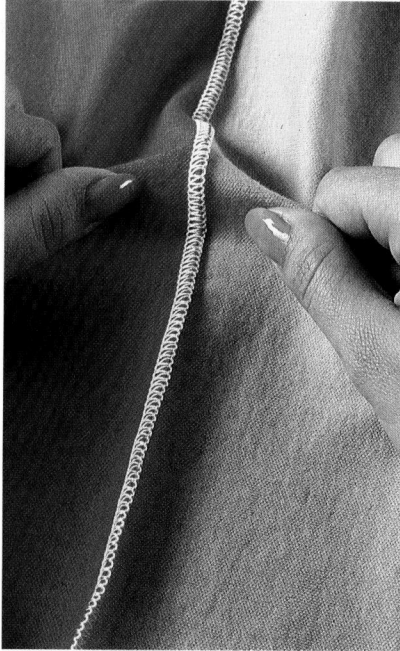

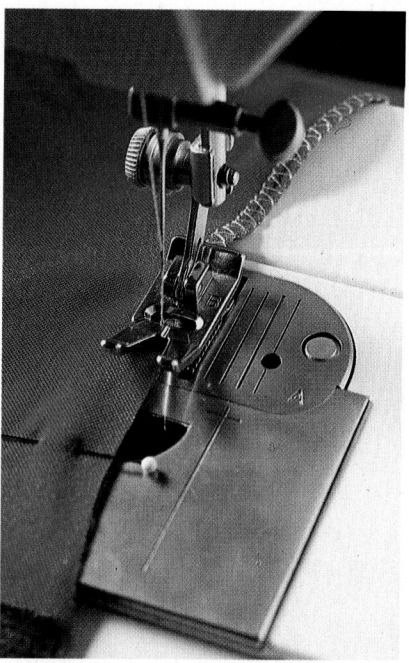

Overlock seam. Use 3-thread overlock stitch on knit fabrics. Seam has a great deal of stretch because of the unique way that the overlock machine loops threads to form stitches. Overlock stitches also help to secure yarn floats on patterned knits.

Flatlock seam. Use 2-thread overlock as decorative seam on right side of garment. Stitch *wrong* sides together; then gently pull seam flat. This seam may also be used on bulky sweater knits or tricot for flat inside seam; stitch with right sides together.

Overedge stretch stitch. Special stretch stitch patterns, such as overedge stitch, are made on reverse-action sewing machines. These seams are strong, elastic, and most appropriate for heavy stress areas, such as armholes and crotch.

Stabilizing Seams

Although most special sewing techniques for knits are designed to maintain the natural stretch in the fabric, it is equally important to use sewing methods that limit the stretch. Use these methods to stay a seam permanently, either to preserve its shape, make it durable, or prevent the knit fabric from stretching. Stabilize seams at shoulders, neckline, and waist.

Four Ways to Stabilize Seams on Knits

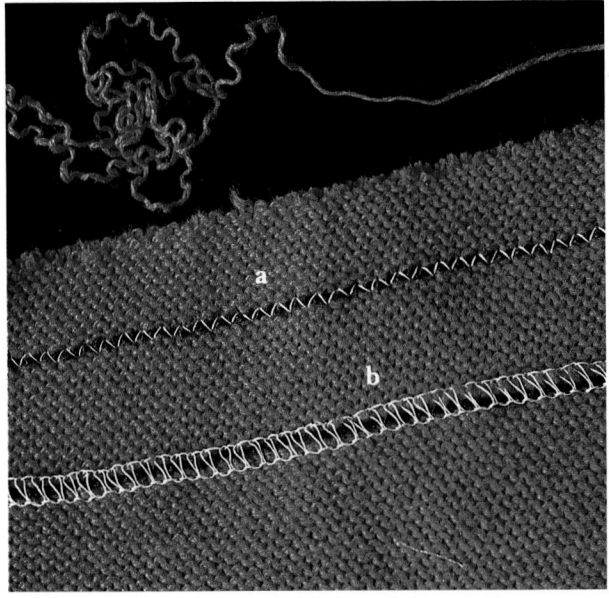

With yarn. For sweater knit, obtain color-matched yarn for seam stay by unraveling scrap of fabric. Steam yarn to straighten it, place yarn on seamline, and zigzag **(a)** or serge **(b)** over yarn.

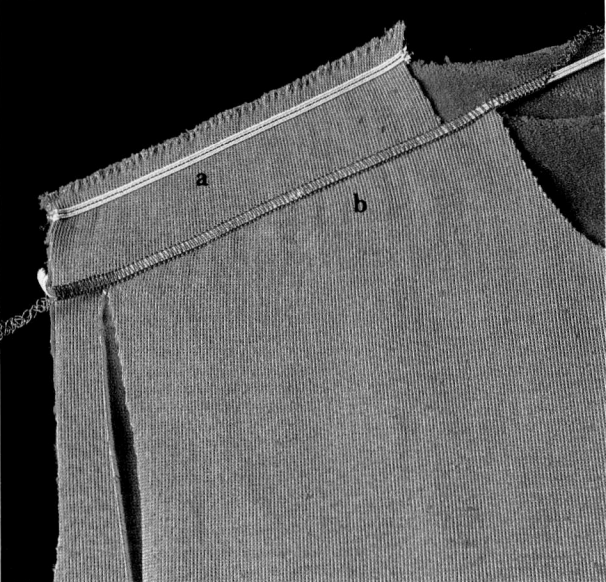

With elastic. Straight-stitch ⅛" (3 mm) elastic **(a)** to seam of two-way stretch knit, stretching elastic and knit slightly as you sew. Elastic allows seam to stretch under stress, then recover to original length. On overlock machine, set stitch width wide enough to overedge the elastic **(b)**.

By topstitching. Press seam allowances to one side. From right side, topstitch close to seamline through garment and seam allowances. Use on lightweight single knits with plain, flat textures.

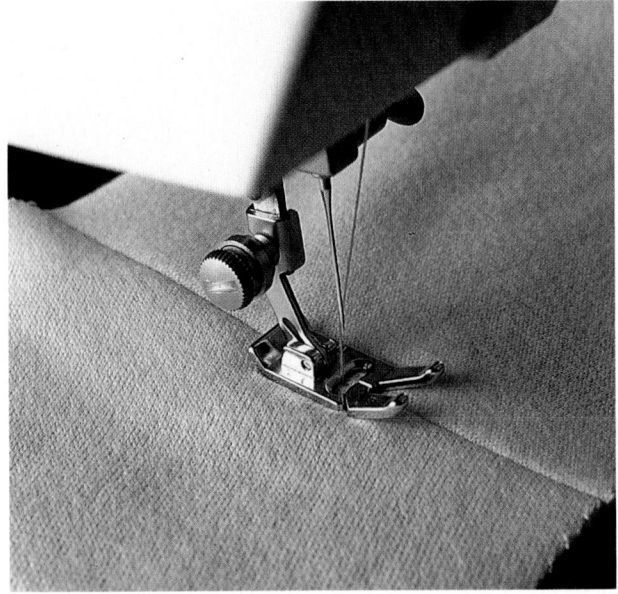

By stitching in the ditch. Press seam open. Working from right side of garment, stitch in the ditch of seam. Use regular stitch length. This method reinforces stable knit seams.

Hems

Inconspicuous hems on knits may be sewn by hand with a catchstitch or by blindstitching on a conventional or overlock machine. On many knit garments, however, the hem does not need to be invisibly sewn. Twin-needle stitching, topstitching, and zigzagging are sturdy and functional for sportswear. To prevent a rippled edge when zigzagging a hem, stitch without stretching.

Five Ways to Hem Knits

Catchstitch. Hand method uses catchstitch, which has built-in give to stretch with the knit. Staystitch raw edge of hem. To hem, work from left to right; take small backstitches alternately at hem edge and through garment. Space stitches ¼" (6 mm) apart, and keep them loose.

Blindstitch. Use stretch blindstitch setting on sewing machine. To stitch, fold hem up, then back on itself. Position work so garment only catches periodically in deeper zigzag stitch. Open out completed hem, and press flat. Stitches easily embed in knit texture for inconspicuous hem.

Overlock blindstitch. Use 2-thread overlock. Fold hem up, then back on itself. Disengage cutting blade, and stitch so overlock stitches catch garment at the same time they overedge hem. Follow same procedure with 3-thread overlock for a simulated band hem.

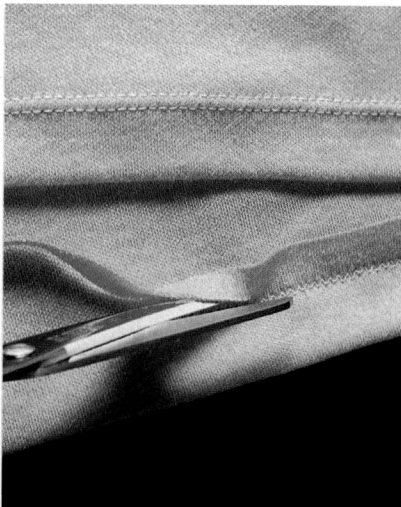

Twin-needle stitching. Turn hem up, and stitch through both layers from right side of garment, using twin needle. Trim excess hem allowance close to stitching. Twin needle produces two parallel lines of topstitching on right side and zigzag stitch on wrong side.

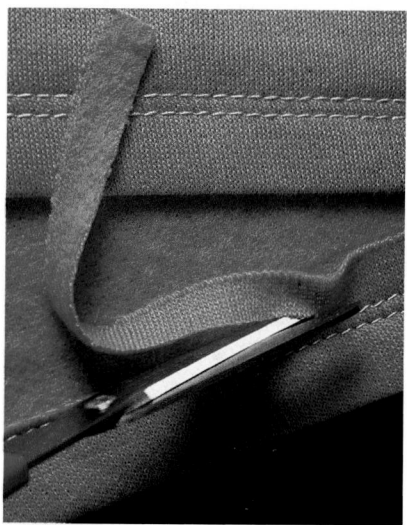

Topstitching. Turn hem up, and topstitch desired distance from hem fold. A second row of topstitching can be added as design detail, which also keeps raw edge from curling. Trim excess hem allowance close to last row of topstitching. Topstitch with buttonhole twist and longer stitch.

Edge Finishes

Edges on knit garments may be finished with ribbing **(1)**, banding **(2),** or narrow binding **(3)**. For ribbing, use purchased tubular ribbing or a stretchy rib knit cut to fit. Bands and binding can be made from self-fabric, or use a contrasting color to create a decorative trim.

Ribbing

Ribbed knits and ribbing vary in how much they stretch. The more the ribbing stretches, the smaller it can be cut to fit a neckline, wrist, or ankle edge on a garment. For this reason, use a ribbing pattern piece as a general cutting guide only.

Custom-cut the ribbing before stitching it to the garment by pin-fitting the ribbing on your figure. For example, if using ribbing for a turtleneck, fold the ribbing around your neck to check the fit. The ribbing must be long enough to slip easily over your head. Allow an extra ½" (1.3 cm) for a ¼" (6 mm) seam to join the ends of the ribbing.

If no pattern piece is given for ribbing, you can add this edge finish to a garment on your own, and there are some general guidelines to follow. Measure the garment edge to be finished with ribbing. If finishing a neck opening, cut the ribbing the measurement of the garment edge plus ½" (1.3 cm) for seam allowances. Adjust the length by pin-fitting. If the ribbing for a pullover opening stretches a great deal,

cut it three-fourths the length of the garment edge plus ½" (1.3 cm) for seam allowances; this gives a snugger fit. If finishing a large garment opening, such as a V-neckline or the waist edge of a sweater, cut the ribbing two-thirds the length of the garment edge plus ½" (1.3 cm) for seam allowances. Custom-fit the ribbing to wrist or ankle cuffs by cutting the ribbing to comfortably fit the body measurements.

Banding

Wide bands, cut crosswise for maximum stretch, can substitute for ribbing if you cannot find a ribbing color match for a garment. For neck openings, use a knit that stretches at least 25 percent crosswise for the bands; 10" (25.5 cm) of knit must stretch to at least 12½" (32 cm). Cut the banding the measurement of the garment edge; then adjust the length by pin-fitting the banding as for ribbing. Allow ½" (1.3 cm) for seam allowances. To finish edges of a cardigan with banding, cut banding to fit garment edge plus hem allowance.

Narrow Binding

Narrow binding can be used instead of a facing or hem on necklines, sleeveless armholes, and sleeves. Because self-binding is not as stretchy as ribbing, use a binding on garment edges that have a zipper or other closure, or on openings large enough to need no closure. This type of binding lies flattest when the finished width is ½" (1.3 cm) or less.

How to Apply Tubular Ribbing

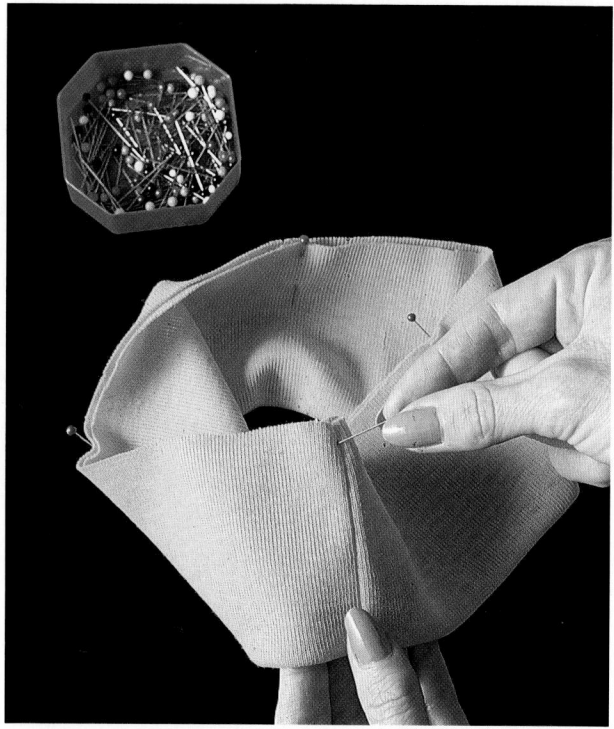

1) Stitch ends of ribbing together in ¼" (6 mm) seam. Fold ribbing in half, wrong sides together. Divide ribbing into four equal parts with pins, placing one pin at ¼" (6 mm) seam on ribbing.

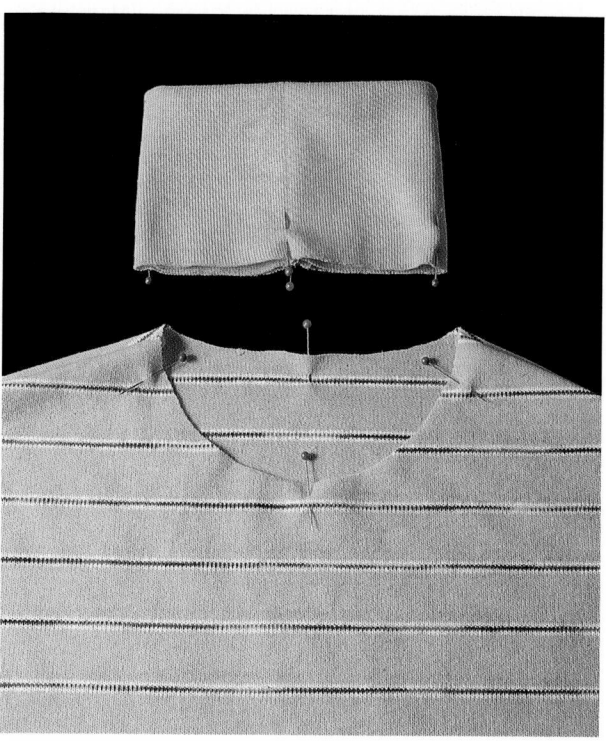

2) Trim seams on garment to ¼" (6 mm), and divide into four equal parts, placing one pin at center back and one at center front; space other pins at halfway points in between.

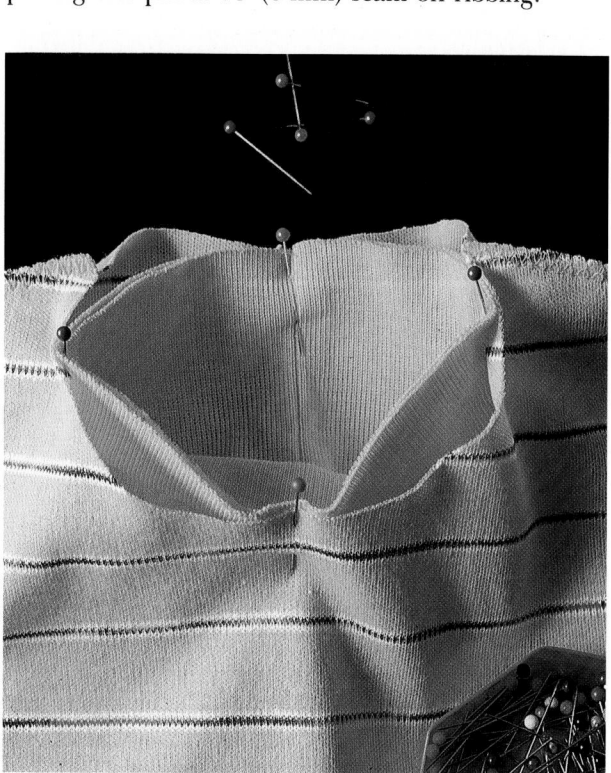

3) Match pin markers on ribbing to garment. Place seam on ribbing at center back of garment.

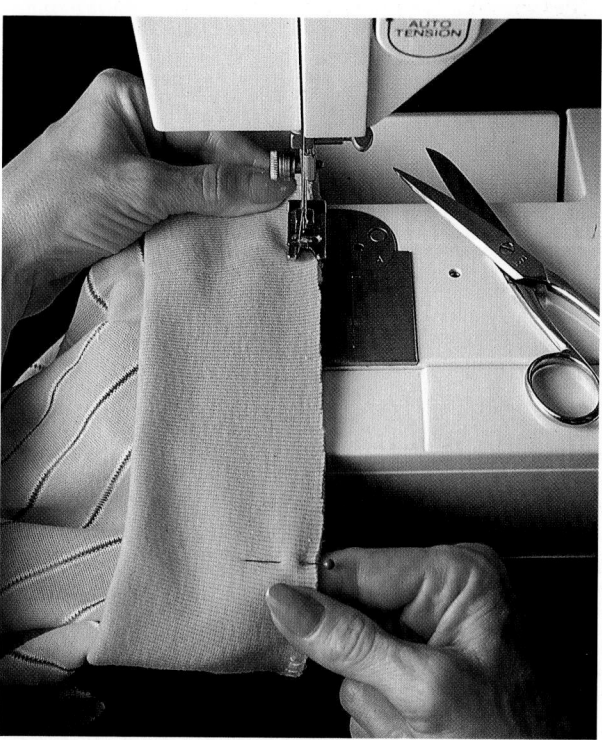

4) Stitch ¼" (6 mm) seam with ribbing on top, garment on bottom, using overedge stretch stitch or 3-thread overlock. Stretch ribbing to fit garment edge between each set of pins. Press seam away from ribbing, toward garment.

How to Finish an Edge with Banding

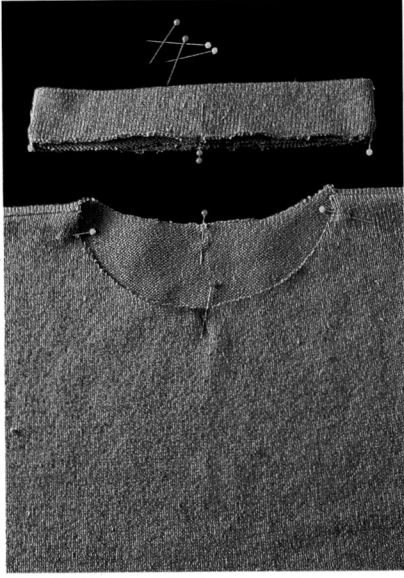

1) Cut band on crosswise or most stretchy direction of knit, twice desired finished width plus ½" (1.3 cm) for seam allowances. Cut band to fit garment edge plus ½" (1.3 cm). Pin band to edge and check fit. For tighter fit, cut band smaller. For neck or sleeve opening, join short ends in ¼" (6 mm) seam.

2) Fold band in half lengthwise, with wrong sides together. Divide band and garment edge into four parts; mark as for tubular ribbing, page 115, step 1. Trim garment seam allowance to ¼" (6 mm) if pattern is not specially designed for knits with ¼" (6 mm) seams.

3) Match markers on band and garment to stitch ¼" (6 mm) seam. Stitch with band on top, garment on bottom, stretching band to fit garment between each set of marking pins.

How to Finish an Edge with Narrow Binding

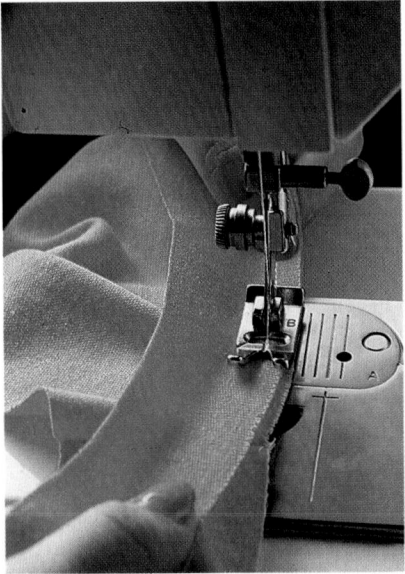

1) Cut binding four times desired finished width. Length should be the measurement of garment edge plus an amount equal to twice the cut width. Trim seam allowances from garment.

2) Stitch binding to garment edge, right sides together, using seam allowance equal to finished width of binding. On inside curve, stretch binding as you sew so binding will lie flat when finished. Leave binding free at beginning and end of seam for finishing.

3) Fold one end of binding diagonally away from garment. Overlap other end, and pin at exact cut width of binding; mark diagonal stitching line between pins. Trim seam allowance to ¼" (6 mm); stitch seam.

4) Press seam allowances away from band, toward garment. From right side, stitch close to seamline, stitching through garment and seam allowances. Stretch fabric slightly as you stitch.

Alternative method for finishing an open-ended band. After cutting band, fold right sides together and stitch ¼" (6 mm) seam on short ends. Turn band right side out. Match ends of band to foldline of hemmed garment. Join band to garment in ¼" (6 mm) seam, stretching band slightly to fit curves. Press and stitch as in step 4.

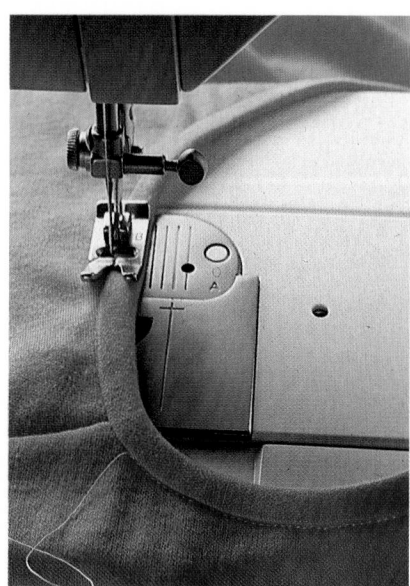

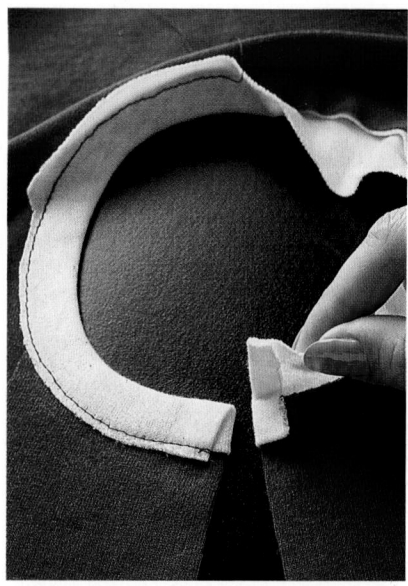

4) Press short diagonal seam open. Finish stitching binding to garment. Press binding and seam allowances away from garment. Fold binding over raw edges.

5) Stitch in the ditch of seam to complete binding, working from right side of garment. Trim close to stitching.

Alternative method for finishing an opening. Attach binding. Finish ends of binding by trimming short ends so they fold around opening ½" (1.3 cm). Fold ends to wrong side of garment, mitering slightly. Finish as in step 5.

Elasticized Waistbands & Cuffs

Complement the stretch in knits by making a comfortable, elasticized waistband on pull-on pants and skirts. The traditional method for adding elastic to the waist of a garment is threading the elastic through a self-fabric casing. For a sportier look, use three or more rows of ½" (1.3 cm) elastic in a wide casing. The same sewing technique used for waistbands can be also used for elasticized cuffs at wrists and ankles. The multiple rows of elastic can be adapted to any pattern by cutting a casing as an extension of the garment.

Elastic will not twist or roll when it is stitched directly to the fabric. With this stitched-on method,

How to Sew a Waistband with Multiple Rows of Elastic

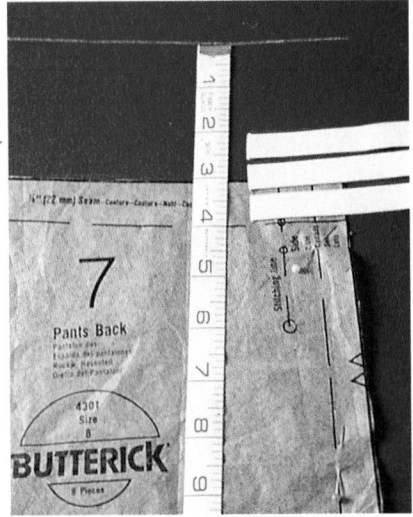

1) Measure casing above natural waistline. For each row of elastic, add the width of the elastic plus ⅛" (3 mm) for ease. Double this amount for the facing; add ¼" (6 mm) for seam allowance. Elastic shown is ½" (1.3 cm) wide.

2) Stitch garment seams, leaving one seam open in facing area. Press under facing on foldline at upper edge of extension.

3) Stitch facing to garment ¼" (6 mm) from raw edge. Stitch two more rows, ⅝" (1.5 cm) apart to form three tunnels for elastic.

How to Apply Stitched-on Elastic to a Waistline Casing

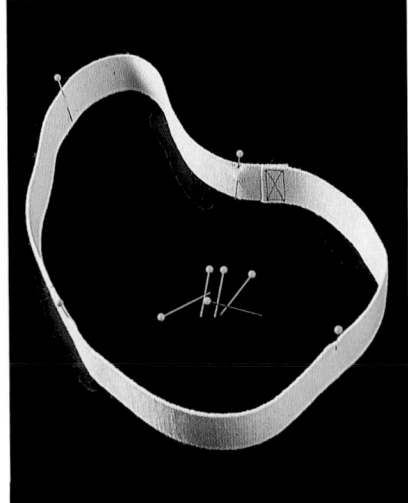

1) Cut elastic slightly smaller than waist measurement. Overlap ends. Stitch ends together to form a circle. Divide elastic into four equal parts, and mark with pins.

2) Cut waistband casing of garment the width of the elastic. Divide garment edge into four equal parts, and mark with pins.

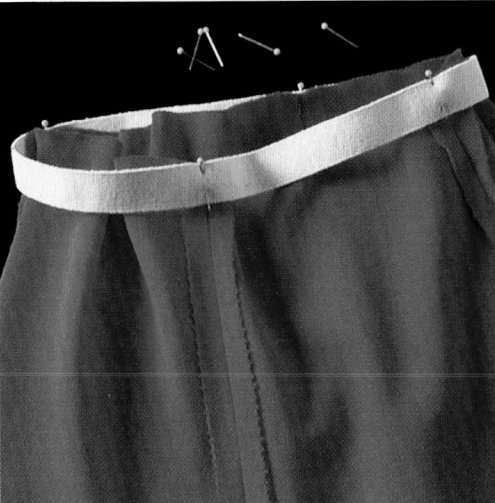

3) Pin elastic to wrong side of garment with edge of elastic even with the edge of the fabric, matching pins.

the facing portion of the self-fabric casing is trimmed off for a neat, nonbulky finish.

Select an appropriate elastic for the application you prefer. For either the casing or the stitched-on method, use a strong woven or knit elastic, which does not become narrower when stretched. Do not use a braided elastic for the stitched-on method. The rubber in braided elastic breaks when pierced by the sewing machine needle. Also, this elastic narrows when stretched, making stretch-as-you-sew techniques difficult. Any type of elastic can be used if you are inserting it in a self-fabric casing the traditional way; non-roll elastic with vertical ribs is an excellent choice because the finished waistband does not twist. Before joining the ends of the elastic, try on the waistband to make sure it slips comfortably over your hips.

4) Use a bodkin or safety pin to insert ½" (1.3 cm) elastic in each tunnel. Overlap elastic ends, and machine-stitch. Slip elastic back into casing. Adjust fullness.

5) Stitch in the ditch at each vertical seam to keep the elastic from rolling or twisting.

6) Adjust gathers. Multiple rows of elastic can be used at waistline or cuffs for comfortable, easy fit.

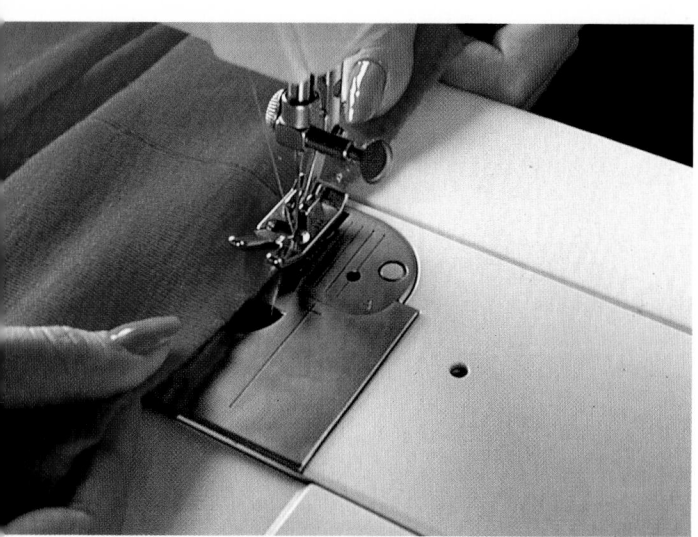

4) Zigzag, overlock, or straight-stitch elastic to edge of garment, stretching elastic to fit as you sew.

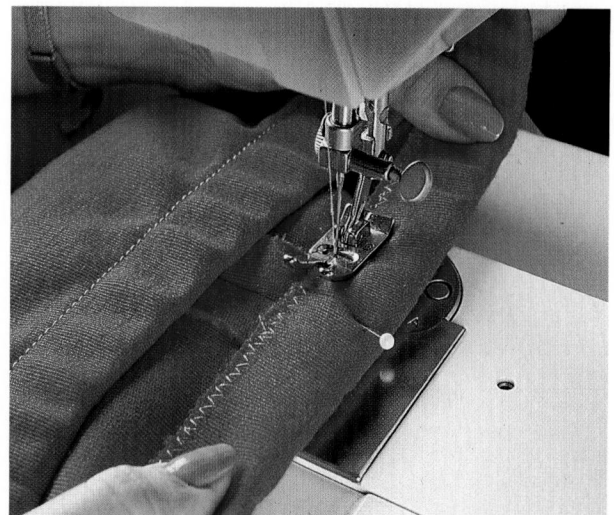

5) Fold garment and elastic to inside; pin. Stitch with narrow zigzag or straight stitch close to inner edge of elastic, stretching the elastic as you sew.

Plackets

The sport collar with a set-in buttoned placket is a popular casual look. For the most professional results, use a prefinished knit collar for this technique.

Compare the depth of the purchased collar to the collar pattern piece. If necessary, trim along the shaped edge of the collar; this edge is seamed to the garment. (The straight, prefinished edge of the collar is the outer edge.) The collar can be stretched to fit the garment neckline during application if it is not as long as the pattern piece.

Work machine-made buttonholes with the machine set at a longer stitch length than the satin stitch, which is used for buttonholes on woven fabrics. If stitches are too closely spaced, the thread piles up and the buttonhole edges look stretched and uneven.

Tips for Buttonholes on Knits

Stabilize buttonhole location with lightweight fusible interfacing. Or use tear-away stabilizer or tissue paper under buttonholes to prevent knit from stretching. Mark buttonhole placement on transparent tape.

Stitch buttonhole parallel to knit ribs for neatest, most even machine-sewn buttonholes. Buttonholes stitched across ribs can ripple, even on firm, stable double knits. Stitch over transparent tape.

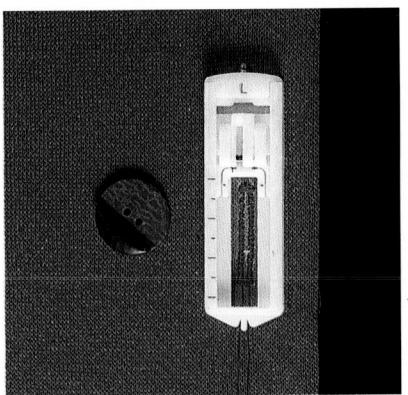

Strengthen buttonhole by stitching over buttonhole twist looped over end of buttonhole foot. After stitching, pull twist through buttonhole; bring twist ends to wrong side, and tie.

How to Sew a Sport Collar and Placket

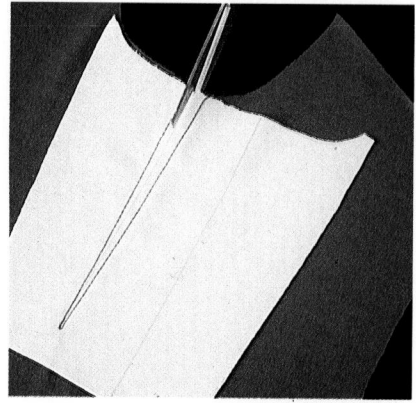

1) Stitch facing to garment front on placket opening marks, right sides together; taper stitching to a point at bottom of opening. (Facing is backed with fusible tricot interfacing.) Slash opening between stitched lines.

2) Turn facing to wrong side of garment. Press right-hand side of opening on seam, rolling the facing slightly to inside. Fold left-hand facing back on placket foldline, and press. Press seam allowances toward placket.

3) Topstitch 1" by ¼" (2.5 cm by 6 mm) open-ended rectangle at bottom of slit. Sew through all layers. Stitch shoulder seams.

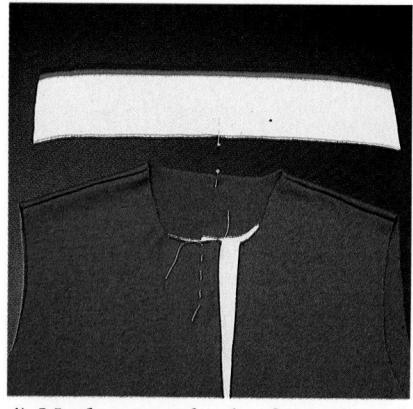

4) Mark center back of purchased collar on shaped edge. Match to center back of garment. Match front edges of collar to garment center front.

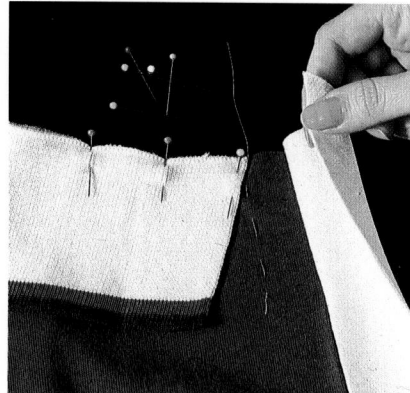

5) Pin collar to right side of garment. Fold facing back over collar on each side of placket opening; pin.

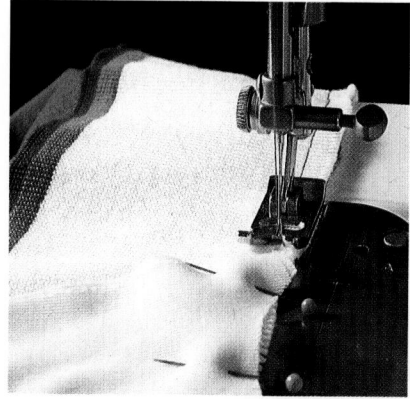

6) Stitch collar to neck edge of garment in ¼" (6 mm) seam. Trim diagonally across corners at placket opening.

7) Turn facing right side out. Press seam allowance toward garment. From right side, topstitch with twin needle, positioning right-hand needle in the ditch of the neck seam; start and end stitching at facing edges.

8) Zigzag seam allowances together in collar area if twin-needle topstitching was not used. Make buttonholes in overlap; sew buttons to underlap.

Two-way Stretch Knits

Two-way stretch knits are designed especially for active sportswear such as swimsuits, dance wear, and aerobic exercise outfits. As knits, they are remarkable because they stretch from 50 percent to 100 percent in both the crosswise and lengthwise directions. Because of the strong, resilient spandex fibers, these fabrics recover to their original dimensions after they have been stretched.

Selecting Patterns

Use these special knits for closely fitted garments sewn from patterns labeled "for use with two-way stretch knits." These patterns are sized to take advantage of two-way stretch knit properties and have little, if any, ease. In many styles, pattern pieces will measure less than your corresponding figure measurements because the garment is supposed to stretch to hug the body closely.

Basic Stitching Techniques

Stretch stitches made by reverse-action sewing machines are strong, elastic, and most appropriate for seams on two-way stretch knits. These stitches are formed by a combination of the back-and-forth and side-to-side movement of the feed dog. By building plenty of thread into a seam and using multiple stitches, the machine creates a finished seam that is able to take stress without breaking the stitches. Do not use the special stretch stitches if they are too close together and use so much thread that the seam is stiff.

Seams sewn on the three-thread overlock machine also are flexible and able to stretch with the fabric in these stress seams.

Consult your sewing machine manual for specific information about sewing with stretch stitches. Most stretch seams require trimming seam allowances to ¼" (6 mm) before sewing unless you are stitching on an overlock machine that stitches and trims in one step. Also, because these stitches are difficult to remove without snagging the fabric, machine-baste the garment together for a try-on fitting before permanently stitching. Make any adjustments before finishing with special stretch stitches or overlocking.

The double-stitched seam is a strong, elastic seam that can be sewn with straight or zigzag stitches. Stretch the fabric as you sew. Test your stretching technique on scraps before starting. To achieve a satisfactory seam, you will need to find the right degree of stretch to incorporate into the seam.

Edges of two-way stretch knit garments are often elasticized to keep them fitted close to the body. When sewing swimwear, use elastic that retains its stretch when wet and resists deterioration from chlorine and other pool chemicals. Some elastics are specially made for swimwear; cotton, polyester, or nylon braid elastics and nylon web or polyester knits are suitable. Acetate elastic is not appropriate because it relaxes when wet.

The stitched-on method for applying elastic gives the most professional results. If the pattern directions are for an elastic inserted in a casing, modify the pattern by selecting elastic that is half the width of the casing provided in the pattern. Cut the casing as instructed in the pattern. Some of the special two-way stretch knit patterns include the stitched-on technique.

To adapt the instructions for other garment edges, such as armholes, necklines, or waistlines, cut the elastic the length of the garment edge minus 1" to 2" (2.5 to 5 cm) for a snug fit. Divide the elastic and garment edge into equal parts before stitching the elastic to the garment. Follow instructions for the swimsuit/leotard leg opening.

How to Judge Double-stitched Test Seams

Seam stretches to degree appropriate to stretch in knit and has neat, even appearance when relaxed. These results come from proper degree of stretching as seam is stitched.

Stitches break when fabric is stretched. This indicates you need to stretch two-way knit to greater degree as you sew double-stitched seam, or seams in garment are likely to split.

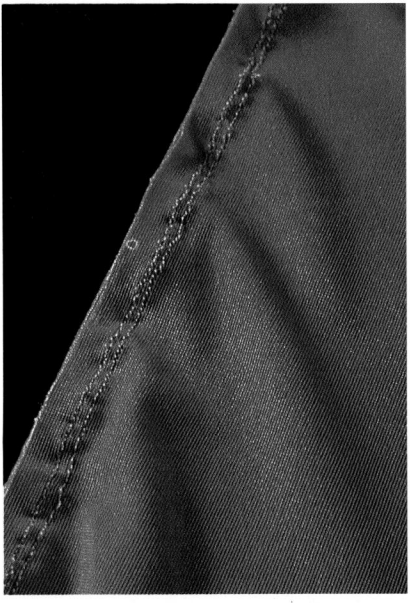

Seam ripples when fabric is relaxed, indicating knit was stretched too much as it was sewn. Overstretching results in too many stitches per inch (2.5 cm). Use slightly longer stitch, and stretch less while stitching.

How to Apply Elastic to a Swimsuit or Leotard Leg Opening

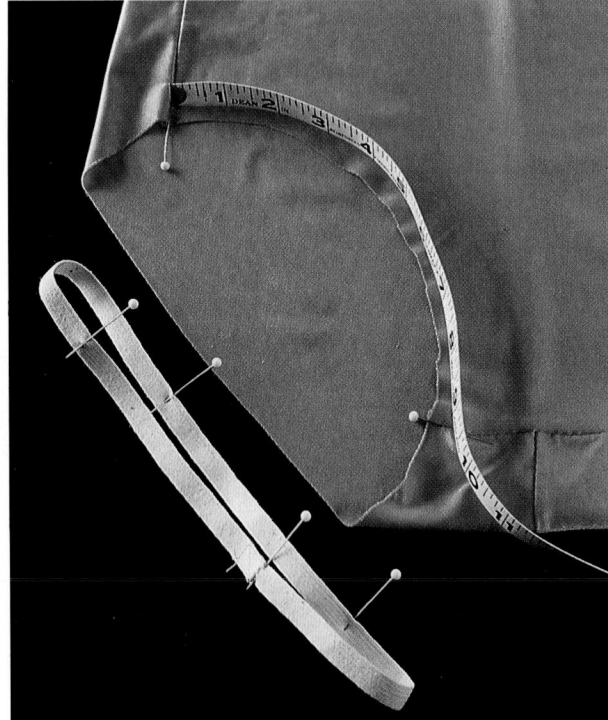

1) Divide elastic circle into four equal parts with pin markers. (Elastic is cut the length of garment opening, minus one-fourth of distance between side and crotch seams in back for leg openings.)

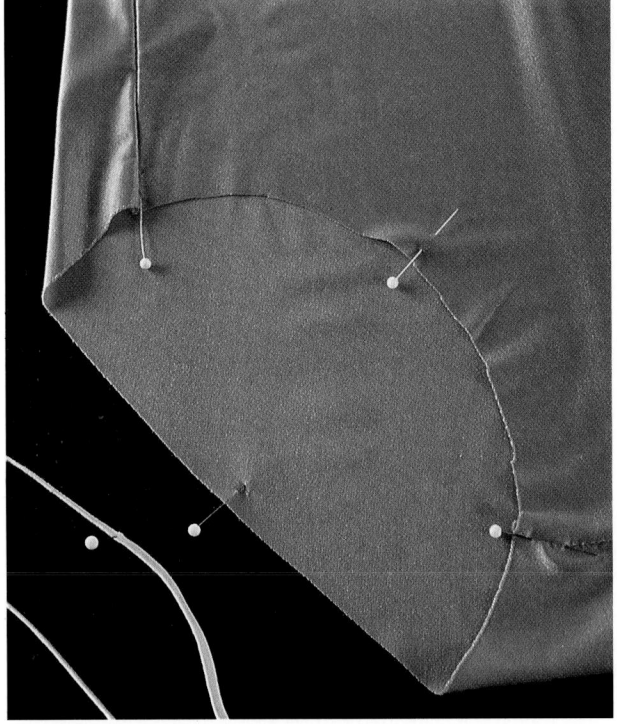

2) Divide leg opening into four *unequal* parts by putting one marker at side seam, one at crotch seam, and one marker halfway in between on front and back. (On neckline and armholes, divide garment edge equally into four parts.)

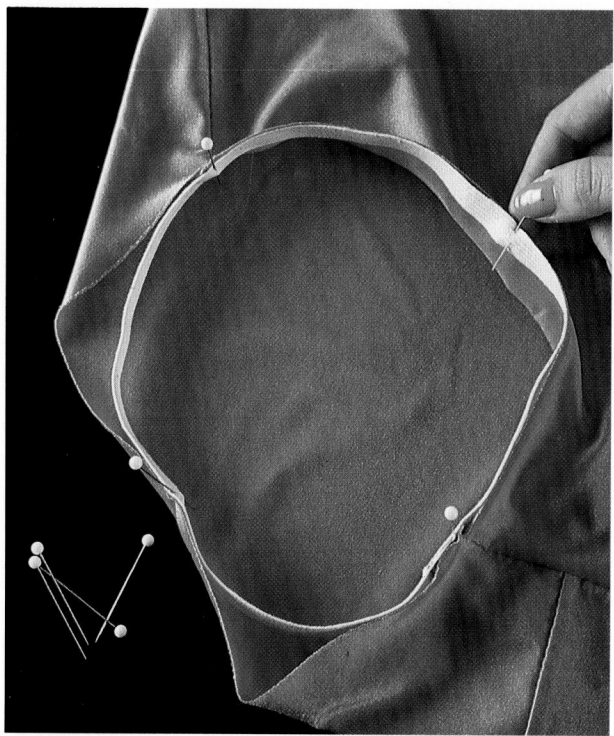

3) Pin elastic to wrong side of garment with edge of elastic even with cut edge. Match pin markers. Because of unequal division on garment, back of leg opening has more fabric than front so swimsuit or leotard fits better over figure contours.

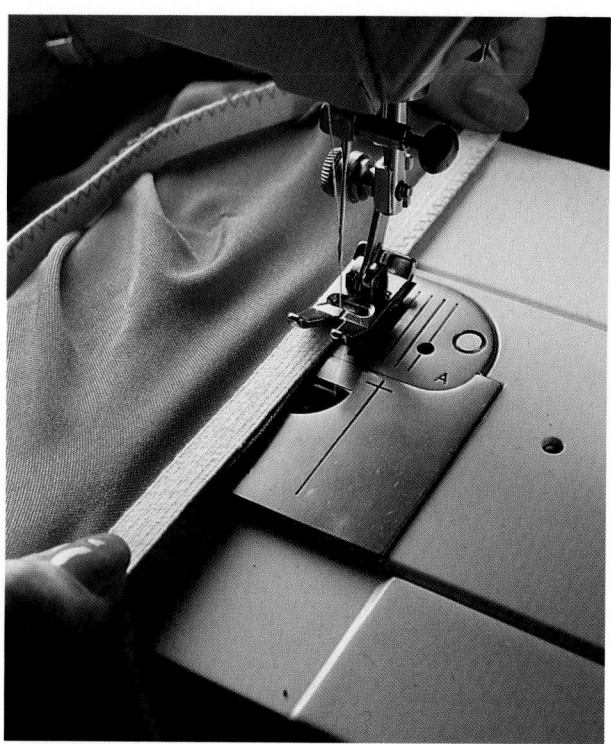

4) Stitch on outside edge of elastic. Use a stretch stitch or narrow zigzag on conventional machine, or 3-thread overlock with cutting blade disengaged.

5) Fold elastic over, toward inside of garment, covering elastic with garment fabric.

6) Stitch over previous stitching, right side of garment up, stretching as you sew. Straight-stitch or zigzag through all layers ¼" (6 mm) from edge. Loosen tension slightly, and stretch as you sew.

Index

A

Accessories, sewing machine, 12-13
Even Feed™ foot, 13, 25, 94
narrow hemmer foot, 13, 36, 39
needles, 12-13
overedge foot, 13
roller foot, 13
special-purpose foot, 13
straight-stitch foot, 13, 25
straight-stitch throat plate, 13, 25
zipper foot, 13
Appliquéd hem, 50
Appliquéd lace, 52

B

Ballpoint needle, 12, 110
Banding, 114, 116-117
Basting tape, 94
Beading, see: lace
Bent-handled shears, 15
Bindings, 29-31
French, 29-31
narrow, 114, 116-117
on buttonholes, 92, 98, 100, 102-103
self-fabric, 31
tricot, 31, 33
Blindstitched hem, 65, 113
Bound, see: bindings
Braid,
elastic, 119
horsehair, 51, 55
soutache braid loops, 56-57
Butted seams, 87
Button loops, 56-57
Buttonhole cutter, 15
Buttonholes,
bound, 92, 98, 100, 102-103
on knits, 120-121
on sheer & silky fabrics, 34-35
on synthetic suede fabrics, 92-93, 100-101
on vinyl, 103
slash, 93, 98, 101-103
Buttons,
reinforcing, 101, 103

C

Casing, waistline, 118-119
Catchstitched hem, 55, 65, 67, 71, 113
Chalk marking pencil, 17

Classic fabrics, 60-81
also see: corduroy, diagonal designs, gabardine, large prints, loose weaves, plaids & stripes, velvet, velveteen
choosing patterns, 62-63
textures & designs, 62-63
Cleaning fabrics, see individual fabrics
Closures,
also see: button loops, buttonholes, buttons, snaps, zippers
on knits, 120
on lustrous fabrics, 56-57
on synthetic fur, 89
on synthetic suede, 92-93, 98-101
on uneven stripes, 81
on vinyl, 102-103
Collars,
faced, 96
lapped, 96
matching plaids & stripes, 77
prefinished knit, 120
with plackets, 120-121
Conventional sewing techniques, 90, 92
Corduroy, 63, 66-67
also see: velveteen
Cuffs, 118-119
Cutting equipment, 14-15

D

Diagonal design fabrics, 63, 72-73
Double knits, see: knits
Double-stitched hem, 88
Double-stitched seams, 27, 46, 48, 123-124

E

Ease a set-in sleeve, 33
removing ease, 91
Edges,
also see: hems, seams
elasticized, 123-125
faced, 97
finishes, on lace, 50-51
French binding, 29-31
lace, 44-45
on knits, 114-117
self-fabric binding, 31
tricot binding, 31
Elastic,
braided, 119
cuffs, 118-119
edges, 123-125
non-roll, with vertical ribs, 119
to stabilize seams, 112
waistbands, 118-119
woven or knit, 119
Embroidered fabrics, 43-45
also see: lace & embroidered fabrics
Enclosed seams,
grading, 66-67
overlock hairline, 28

zigzag hairline, 28
Equipment, 12-17
also see: needles, pins, shears, thread
Even & uneven plaids & stripes, 76-81
Even Feed™ foot, 13, 25, 94
Eyelet fabric, 43-45
also see: lace & embroidered fabrics

F

Fabric,
also see individual fabrics
pattern tracing fabric, 14
pressing, 16
Faced hem, 55, 88, 97
Facings, 98-99
also see: interfacings
Finishes, 114-117
also see: bindings, edges, hems, seams
edges on laces, 50-51
French binding, 29-31
hems on lace, 50-51
self-fabric binding, 31
tricot binding, 31
Flat construction method, 90, 93
Flat-fell seams, 65, 103
Flatlock seam, 111
French binding, 29-31
French seam, 26-27
Fringed hem, 65
Fur, see: synthetic fur
Fur hooks & eyes, 89
Fusible,
interfacings, 24, 109
web, 16, 52, 90, 94

G

Gabardine fabrics, 63, 74
Gauge, stretch knit, 108
Glue stick, 94
Grading enclosed seam allowances, 66-67
Gripper snaps, 103

H

Hairline hem, 36-38
Hairline seams, 27-28
Hand-rolled hem, 36-37, 39
Hand steamer, 16
Hand washing silks, 22
Hems, 36-39, 65
blindstitched, 65, 113
catchstitched, 55, 65, 67, 71, 113
double-stitched, 88
faced, 55, 88, 97
finishes, on lace, 50
fringed, 65
hairline, 36-38
hand-rolled, 36-37, 39

hemming-foot, 36-37, 39
horsehair braid, 51, 55
overlock blindstitch, 113
overlocked edge, 36-37, 67
rolled overlocked, 36-37
straight, 97
topstitched, 36, 38, 55, 65, 103, 113
tricot-bound, 36-37, 65
twin-needle stitching, 113
Hong Kong underlining, 29, 32
Hooks & eyes, 89
Horsehair braid hem, 51, 55

I

Insertions, see: lace
Interfacings, 24
  for delicate fabrics, 24
  hidden plackets, 34-35
  in knits, 109
  in sequined & metallic fabrics, 58
  in synthetic suede, 90
  in velvet, 70
  in vinyl, 102-103
  on collars, 96
  preshrinking, 22
Iron soleplate cover, 16
Ironing, see: pressing

K

Knife blade cutting tool, 15
Knit fusible interfacing, 24
Knits, 104-125
  care, 108
  edge finishes, 114-117
  fabric preparation, 108
  hems, 113
  interfacings, 109
  layout, 109
  plackets, 120-121
  pressing, 109
  selecting needle, stitch length &
    thread, 110
  stabilizing seams, 112
  stretch knit gauge, 108
  two-way stretch, 108, 122-125
  types, 107
  waistbands & cuffs, 118-119

L

Lace & embroidered fabrics, 42-52
  appliqués, 52
  care, 46
  fabric preparation, 46
  facings, interfacings, underlinings, 46
  hem & edge finishes, 50-51
  layout & cutting, 46-47
  pressing, 46
  seams, 48-49
  types, 43-45

Lapped collar & facing, 96
Lapped seams, 46, 48-49, 90, 93,
  95, 99
Lapped zippers, 99
Large print fabrics, 62, 75
Layout, 11
  also see individual fabrics
  equipment, 14-15
Leather, see: vinyl
Linings, 22, 24, 29-31, 46
Liquid marker, 25
Loops,
  button, 57
  mock button, 56
  soutache braid, 56-57
  tape, 57
Loose weave fabrics, 62, 64-65
Lustrous fabrics, 53-59
Lustrous velvets, 68

M

Marking, 17, 25
  also see individual fabrics
Masking tape, 15
Matching plaids & stripes, 77, 79-81
Metallic fabrics, see: sequined &
  metallic fabrics
Mock buttonloop closure, 56

N

Narrow binding, 114, 116-117
Narrow hem, see: hems
Narrow hemmer foot, 13
Narrow zigzag seams, 46, 111
Needle board, 16
Needles, 12, 110
  ballpoint, 12, 110
  for knits, 110
  for laces, 43
  for lustrous fabrics, 54
  for silkies, 21
  for synthetic fur, suede & leather, 85
  sharp point, 12
  twin, 12
  universal point, 12, 110
Nonwoven fusible interfacing, 24, 109
Nonwoven sew-in interfacing, 24

O

Overedge foot, 13
Overedge stretch stitch, 111-112
Overlock blindstitch hem, 113
Overlocked hem, 36-37
Overlocked seam, 48, 65
  enclosed hairline, 28
  French, 27
  in knits, 111-112

P

Panne, 68
Patch pocket, see: pocket
Pattern tracing fabric, 14
Patterns,
  adapting, 91
  layout, 11, 14-15
  selection, 10-11
    for corduroy & velveteen, 66
    for diagonal designs, 72
    for gabardine, 74
    for knits, 107-109, 123
    for lace & embroidered fabrics,
      44-46
    for large prints, 75
    for loose weave fabrics, 64
    for plaids & stripes, 76-77
    for sequined & metallic fabrics, 58
    for sheer & silky fabrics, 22-23
    for synthetic fur, 86
    for synthetic suede, 90
    for velvet, 69
    for vinyl, 102
Pins, 14-15
Plackets, 34-35
  buttonholes, 35
  on knits, 120-121
Plaids & stripes, 64, 76-81
  even & uneven patterns, 76, 78-81
  layout, cutting & marking, 76-78
Pockets,
  in plaids, 77, 79
  patch, 92-93
Point presserclapper, 16
Preshrinking,
  corduroy, 66
  interfacing, 22, 24, 90
  knits, 108
  lace & embroidered fabrics, 46
  linings, 22
  loose weave fabric, 64
  sheer & silky fabrics, 22-23
  velveteen, 66
Press cloth, 16
Pressing, 16
  also see individual fabrics

R

Remove ease from set-in sleeve
  pattern, 91
Repeat of pattern, 76-77
Ribbing, 107, 114-115
Rolled overlocked hem, 36-37
Roller foot, 13
Rotary cutter, 15

S

Satin, see: lustrous fabrics
Seam roll, 16
Seams, 26-28, 48-49
  butted, 87

Seams (continued)
  curved, 70
  double-stitched, 27, 46, 48, 123-124
  enclosed overlocked hairline, 28
  enclosed zigzag hairline, 28
  flat-fell, 65, 103
  flatlock, 111
  French, 26-27
  grading enclosed, 66-67
  hairline, 27-28
  in knits, 111-112
  lapped, 46, 48-49, 90, 93, 95, 99
  matching pattern, 73, 81
  narrow zigzag, 46, 111
  on sequined fabrics, 59
  overedge stretch stitch, 111-112
  overlocked, 27, 48, 65, 111-112
  plain, 65, 95, 98, 103
  pressing, 16, 71, 74
  stabilizing, 112
  topstitched, 92, 95, 112
  welt, 92, 95, 103
  zigzag, 46, 111-112
  zippers in, 98-99
Self-fabric,
  binding, 31
  interfacing, 24
  on zippers, 98
Sequined & metallic fabrics, 53, 58-59
Serger, 12
Serrated-edge shears, 15
Set-in sleeves, 33
Sets, 45
  also see: lace
Sewing aids, 12-17
  also see: accessories, equipment
Sewing equipment, 12-13
Sewing machine, 12-13, 27
Sharp point needles, 12-13, 110
Shears,
  bent-handled, 15
  serrated-edge, 15
Sheer & silky fabrics, 18-39
  bindings & underlinings, 29-31
  fabric preparation, 22-23
  interfacings, 24
  guide to sewing, 21
  hems, 36-39
  hidden plackets, 34-35
  layout & cutting, 23
  marking & stitching, 25
  pressing, 22
  seams, 26-28
Silicone lubricant, 13, 94
Silk-covered snaps, 89
Silky fabrics, 20-21
  also see: sheer & silky fabrics
  as interfacing, 24
  hand washing, 22
Single-edged razor blade, 15
Slash buttonhole, 93, 98, 101-103
Sleeves,
  ease a set-in, with tricot binding, 33
  remove ease from set-in, 91
  set-in, 91
Smooth-edged tracing wheel, 17
Snaps, 89, 103
Soutache braid loop, 56-57

Special occasion fabrics, 40-59
  also see: lace & embroidered fabrics,
    lustrous fabrics
Special-purpose foot, 13
Stabilizing seams on knits, 112
Stay, waistline, 56
Stitch in the ditch, 31, 112
Stitch length,
  for laces, 43
  for knits, 110
  for lustrous fabrics, 54
  for sheer & silky fabrics, 21
  for synthetic fur, suede & leather, 85
Stitches, 12-13, 25
  overedge stitch, 111, 123
  to prevent skipping, 25
Straight hem, 97
Straight-stitch foot, 13, 25
Straight-stitch throat plate, 13, 25
Stretch as you sew technique, 111
Stretch knit gauge, 108
Stretch nonwoven interfacing, 109
Stretch stitches, 123
Striped fabrics, see: plaids & stripes
Strips, of lace, 45
Suede, see: synthetic suede
Synthetic fibers, 20
Synthetic fur, 84-89
Synthetic leather, see: vinyl
Synthetic suede, 84-85, 90-101
  care, 85
  closures, 92-93, 98-101
  conventional techniques, 92
  flat techniques, 93
  guide to sewing, 85
  hems, 97
  layout, cutting & marking, 90-91
  pressing, 90
  seams, 95

T

Tailor's chalk, 17
Testing,
  a pattern, 10-11, 90
  even pattern of plaids & stripes, 76
  fusible interfacing, 24
  stretchability of knits, 108
Textured knits, 107
Thread, 12-13, 17, 21, 43, 54, 85, 110
Tissue paper, 13
Tools, see: equipment
Topstitched hem, 36, 38, 55, 65,
  103, 113
Topstitched seam, 92, 95, 112
Tracing,
  pattern tracing fabric, 14
  smooth-edged tracing wheel, 17, 25
  with thread, 17
Transparent tape, 17
Tricot binding,
  edge, 31
  hem, 36-37, 65
  in set-in sleeves, 33
Tricot interfacing, 109
Trims,
  appliqués, 52

lace, 44-46
rib knit, 107
Tubular ribbing, 107, 114-115
Twin-needle stitching, 12, 113
Two-way stretch knits, 106-108,
  122-125
  also see: knits

U

Underlinings, 29, 32, 46
Universal point needle, 12, 110

V

Velvet fabrics, 63, 68-71
Velveteen, 63, 66-67
Vinyl, 84-85, 102-103

W

Waistbands, 118-119
Waistline,
  casing, 118-119
  stays, 56
Wales, corduroy, 66
Web, see: fusible web
Weights, 15
Welt seams, 92, 95, 103
"With nap" pattern layout,
  corduroy, 63
  gabardine, 63
  knits, 109
  lace, 46
  lustrous fabric, 54
  plaids & stripes, 76
  synthetic suede, 90
Woven interfacing, 24

Y

Yarn, to stabilize seams, 112

Z

Zigzag seams, 46, 111-112
Zipper foot, 13
Zippers,
  centered, 98
  in synthetic fur, 89
  in synthetic suede, 98
  in vinyl, 102-103
  lapped, 99
  prickstitched, 56
  with waistline stay, 56